# Tax and Financial Planni
# for Sportsmen and Entertainers

# Tax and Financial Planning for Sportsmen and Entertainers

Second Edition

Richard Baldwin BCom, FCA, ATII
Tax Partner
Touche Ross

Richard Harvey FCA, TEP
Tax Partner
Stoy Hayward

*Print on Demand Edition*

Tottel
publishing

**Published by**
**Tottel Publishing Ltd**
**Maxwelton House**
**41-43 Boltro Road**
**Haywards Heath**
**West Sussex**
**RH16 1BJ**

ISBN 13: 978-1-84592-753-0
ISBN 10: 1-84592-753-2

First published 1989
Second edition 1994
Formerly published by LexisNexis Butterworths

This edition reprinted by Tottel Publishing Ltd 2007



**British Library Cataloguing-in-Publication Data.**
A catalogue record for this book is available from the British Library.

Typeset by Kerrypress Ltd, Luton, Bedfordshire
Printed and bound in Great Britain by
Marston Book Services, Abingdon, Oxfordshire

# Acknowledgments

The Inland Revenue Forms P11D and 46R-1 and the FEU Payers Guide reproduced in Appendices V, VI and VII are Crown copyright and are reproduced with the kind permission of the Controller of HMSO.

# Preface

The intention of this book is to outline the UK income tax position of entertainers and sportsmen (performers), both those resident in the UK and those who, while remaining non-resident, come here to perform. It also sets out to provide a general guide to the overseas taxation position of UK resident individuals who perform in or receive income from certain countries outside the UK. To assist in this, a résumé of the tax position in a number of the main overseas markets has been given, together with a summary of the tax treaty provisions relevant to such individuals.

In many instances, the peak earning period of the entertainer or sportsman is short, with high levels of income in that period. It is therefore essential that all possible steps are taken to maximise the opportunities to produce income in that period and also to mitigate the tax liability on those earnings. In addition to providing a guide to the labyrinth of provisions which need to be taken into account when seeking to mitigate the performer's tax liability, this book also provides some guidelines to ensuring that adequate funds are available to him or her, not only to meet his or her tax liabilities as they fall due but also to ensure that a healthy residue of his or her income remains after his or her career is over.

The authors recognise from practical experience that the problems of agreeing individuals' tax liabilities and planning for their future are frequently compounded by inadequate accounting records and information and we hope that the suggestions contained herein as to the nature of the records which need to be maintained will help other practitioners to avoid these problems.

We would like to thank our colleagues at Stoy Hayward, Touche Ross and Horwath International for their assistance in writing this edition of the book. Special thanks are also due to Angela Dickinson who ensured that the time was available for this edition to be written and for Robert Reed's contribution to Chapter 6 on non-resident performers.

Any errors or omissions are, however, entirely our own. The tax position stated is at 30 April 1994.

Richard Baldwin
Richard Harvey
May 1994

# Contents

# Table of statutes

References in this Table to *Statutes* are to Halsbury's Statutes of England Fourth Edition showing the volume and page at which the annotated text of the Act may be found.

# Table of cases

# Introduction

The purpose of this book is to examine the UK tax position of entertainers and sportsmen and women (which hereafter, unless distinctions are to be made, we will call performers) both those resident in the UK and those who perform here while continuing to be non-resident. The book also provides a résumé of the tax position of UK resident performers who perform in, or receive income from, overseas countries describing briefly the foreign tax position in the major overseas countries of interest to performers. It is frequently assumed that performers are self-employed and while this is often the case, a significant proportion are, in legal terms, employees of a corporate body. The book examines the taxation of performers under both arrangements and discusses the contrasting tax liabilities and planning opportunities provided by each.

The phrase 'entertainers and sportsmen' is wide-ranging. For the purposes of the book, we have taken it to mean individuals whose earnings are derived from the exploitation of their talents for the entertainment of others.

Performers participate in many ways, eg as individuals or as members of teams or groups. In some sports, the athlete is regarded as an amateur and in others he competes as a professional. Many have substantial earnings derived from sources other than direct participation, eg sponsorship, merchandising etc. This book attempts to cover the tax aspects of all of these.

The first chapter deals with financial planning for performers and this is an area of utmost importance. It should be remembered that neither effective financial nor tax planning can be carried out unless the individual has proper accounting records and the chapter includes some guidelines on the nature of the records which should be maintained.

Often, the working life of the performer is short and the pattern of income will be unpredictable. In some cases, income may remain at low levels for many years with a sudden peak, whereas in other cases 'stardom' may be almost immediate. In the case of sportsmen careers can end at a relatively early age and injury can curtail a successful career at any stage. Where the peak earnings are unlikely to continue for a considerable length of time, it is essential that all possible steps are taken to mitigate the tax liability on those earnings and proper provision is made for the individual's future. The professional adviser can assist in ensuring that adequate funds are available to meet both the individual's personal requirements and his tax liabilities as they fall due. Finally, because of the unpredictability of the performer's career development and his income pattern the keynote of advice in this area must be flexibility.

Performers in general are very visible: they give interviews, write for newspapers, appear on stage, television and radio and write books. Inspectors of Taxes are very often keen on sport and entertainment, may take a particular personal interest and build up a significant amount of financial information and knowledge about these activities. As a result, performers, particularly the self-employed and those in the top flight, command greater attention and interest from the Inland Revenue. Unfortunately, however, financial information is often not readily available for the performer, particularly the self-employed and those who have other sources of income, whose tax affairs are often complex. Consequently their tax affairs are in arrears, with returns and accounts not submitted on time even though the amounts of tax due may be substantial. This makes them a prime case for Inland Revenue investigation and, as the cases of Lester Piggott and Ken Dodd illustrate, the Inland Revenue may wish to make examples of such high profile performers. With the advent of self-assessment it will be increasingly important to deal with their affairs accurately and on a timely basis.

## Inland Revenue approach

In recent years, the Inland Revenue has become more investigative than technical, particularly with the increased pressure on it to become cost effective and it has collected significant amounts from these 'compliance' activities. Penalties and interest are automatic when there has been substantial delay on the taxpayer's part and in-depth examination and cross-checking against the many other sources of information have become commonplace. This process will be reinforced by self-assessment when it is introduced in 1996/97.

There have also been changes in the law and practice over the last few years aimed at increasing tax revenue from performers. The Inland Revenue have increasingly sought to classify performers as employees rather than self employed with the effect that tax is collected through the PAYE system and the number of expenses which can be set against the income is dramatically reduced.

The introduction of withholding tax on payments to non-resident performers has also strengthened the Inland Revenue's hand in collecting tax in this area. However, the estimates which were given by the chancellor in the 1986 Budget of collecting £75m in 1987/88 appears to have been wildly optimistic with the actual collection being £6.9m in 1987/88 rising to £19.9m in 1992/93.

While the affairs of non-resident performers will be dealt with by the specialist Foreign Entertainers Unit, the tax affairs of UK resident performers can be dealt with either in a local tax district, which generally has no specialisation in sport or entertainment or by one of the Inland Revenue Special Compliance Offices for the more serious investigation cases. However, Special Office is probably the most important Inland Revenue agency in relation to performers. This is the technical investigation unit which is part of head office and which may get involved where the tax to be collected is substantial or the performer's affairs are complex.

## Inland Revenue Special Compliance Offices

The various Special Compliance Offices spread around the country have undertaken a number of reviews of sectors in the entertainment industry. Solihull Special Office has shown particular interest in the entertainment and sports sectors and the Foreign Entertainers Unit (see p 89) was developed from this office. Footballers, athletes, golfers and tennis players have all been singled out for review. The Inspectors with the various Special Offices have considerable discretion to pursue 'tax leaks' and they are encouraged to develop a complete understanding of a particular sector. Using this knowledge they will then look at the levels of tax which they consider to be lost and try to reach a negotiated settlement. Often, having looked at one problem in a particular geographical location, they may attempt to rectify the situation for the future in other areas rather than go back over prior years. They are likely to continue to monitor the situation to ensure compliance. This was the case in relation to semi-professional football in England where, as the result of discussions with the Edinburgh and Leeds Special Offices, the Football Association put out a circular covering the operation of PAYE on payments made by football clubs. Over the 12 years since the Inland Revenue started their investigations into semi-professional football they have recovered significant amounts of tax, and continue to be unhappy about the situation at many clubs. In the last four years they have extended their interest to professional football and other sports, eg rugby union.

The cases come from a number of sources and there is a significant inflow of information, including formal reporting to the Inland Revenue. It is not unusual for the Special Office to concentrate on the top sportsmen in a particular sport where the potential tax leakage is greatest. Inspectors will often talk to and seek to negotiate a global settlement with the professional league, association or the governing body responsible for a particular sport. They have always got the back-up of technical specialists at Somerset House and, as with the districts, they will often pursue their arguments through the Commissioners and upwards. Particular areas of interest have been self-employed sportsmen, the use of offshore companies, pension contributions and cash payments which are often paid on a tax-free basis in some sports.

## Reporting by performers

There is often a worrying lack of awareness among performers of their tax obligations. The 'amateur' sportsman, in particular, is often not encouraged by his own sports' rules to report his income for tax purposes for fear of being stripped of his right to compete. Indeed, it appears that often sportsmen are more concerned with not breaking the sport's rules rather than returning the income to the Inland Revenue. Tax and financial planning for the amateur sportsman is often characterised by an absence of written agreements and by payments in cash. Notwithstanding that in order to compete in a particular sport the individual must be an amateur, he may still have taxable income to report. One might imagine that help in tax and financial planning is forthcoming from the governing bodies in these circumstances but often it is not.

For the self-employed, tax reporting will involve the drawing up of accounts. In many instances, information is extremely sketchy and the accounts are drawn up some significant time later when it is difficult to ensure that everything is reported. Tax rules themselves are complex and, although the self-employed performer is in great need of an accountant, he is not always prepared to use one. The situation is often not helped by agents who earn substantial commissions but often do not consider the performer's tax reporting obligations. In the current environment of greater penalties and interest for delay, with little sympathy for late returns and an absence of payments on account, reporting is becoming more and more important for high earning performers.

## Guidance for performers

Official guidance within either sport or the entertainment industry to the performer as to how to handle his or her financial and tax affairs is very limited. In sport little has been issued by the sports governing bodies themselves – perhaps because they feel that this is a matter best dealt with by the sportmen's own advisers or professional body. The authors are, however, aware of the following bodies which do provide some help:

(1) The Professional Footballers Association which includes some useful material in its handbook and has other material on tax which is available on request.
(2) In an effort to alert athletes in particular of their tax obligations the Sports Aid Foundation has produced a simple question and answer checklist. This is reproduced as Appendix I.

## Reporting by others

The Inland Revenue gets a significant amount of information on the performer from which it can check the income and expenses reported. This comes from a multitude of sources:

- for those who are employed, from PAYE and P11D reporting;
- TMA 1970 s 16 returns – governing bodies of sport are often required to report payments to international players of fees (this is not confined to players but can include coaches, officials, physiotherapists and managers);
- corporate Inspectors of Taxes dealing with entertainment companies' affairs may request information about its employees, consultants or contracted artists;
- foreign tax authorities;
- governing bodies may provide information concerning funds held on behalf of their sportsmen and details of particular types of payment, eg ex gratia payments;

- information returns are provided by sponsors of performers such as cash payments and gifts provided;
- Forms 46R submitted to the Inland Revenue for media payments and Forms 46R-1 for payments relating to the use of copyright.

The importance of providing full and complete information to the Inland Revenue cannot therefore be over emphasised. This is particularly important in terms of meetings and negotiations with Special Office when the Inspector will often have independent evidence on the accounts which are being submitted. Unfortunately, in some cases the information provided independently is not always accurate, nor are details always retained by those providing it. There have been cases where Special Office have visited the offices of third parties, eg pension scheme advisers, and taken copies of a substantial number of documents for use in their enquiries.

## The scope of the book

The book deals primarily with income taxes, value added tax and national insurance. There is no direct discussion of capital taxes or estate planning unless the implications are a side effect of other planning, eg the use of pensions, turning income into capital etc. We hope that the book will primarily be of interest to the performer's advisers whether they be accountant, solicitor or one of the many professional managers who act for performers. Further, within sport we hope that it will also be of interest to those involved in organising and administering particular sports and sportsmen, eg governing bodies and associations representing performers. The book covers a number of tax planning areas but no strategy as extreme as that carried out by the intergalactic megastar Hotblack Desiato from the group Disaster Area in *The Restaurant at the End of the Universe* whose manager tells Ford Prefect that his star is dead for a year for tax reasons!

# 1 Financial planning

## General principles

Financial planning for performers is in many respects similar in principle to that for individuals in other businesses in that the largest net profits will be achieved by maximising income and controlling expenses. Special considerations do, however, arise for the performer who typically has a short performing life, or who may experience peaks and troughs in income levels due to performing success or lack of it, or who usually receives income from a number of sources or who, in the case of the sportsman, finds that his career ends abruptly due to injury. Financial planning involves more than just maximising business income and effective planning should ensure that, in particular, the performer:

(1) has sufficient disposable income to meet personal expenditure (or otherwise restricts such expenditure);
(2) makes proper provision for the payment of taxes; and
(3) in the long run makes adequate provision for himself after his career has ended.

Planning should take account of the performer's personal objectives. It may be necessary for the performer to borrow in order to meet his short- or long-term financing requirements and often this borrowing will be from a clearing bank or similar institution. The availability and provision of reliable financial information is vital to obtain bank finance and to the financial planning process.

## Financial records and information

It is generally recognised that all types of business require financial information on a regular basis and therefore some form of accounting system needs to be employed. However, performers have often failed in the past to maintain adequate basic records, giving rise to a number of problems, not all of which are tax related eg:

(1) poor control of income receipts may allow overdue or omitted income sources to go undetected;
(2) an inaccurate record of earnings and expenditure and, more importantly, the failure to anticipate future income and expenditure

levels has caused many performers to overspend leaving them unable to meet future liabilities including tax in respect of past earnings;

(3) inaccurate and late tax returns render the taxpayer vulnerable to interest and penalties on overdue tax[1] or, alternatively, to the possibility of the overpayment of tax;

(4) poor records increase the likelihood of an 'in-depth' investigation by the Inland Revenue because of the performer's inability to substantiate his statements of income and expenditure;

(5) failure to comply with the VAT legislation requiring the maintenance of proper VAT records which can result in interest and penalties.

This chapter highlights the particular problems that can arise for performers and the ways in which they may be avoided or overcome. The accounting records required will depend on the size and complexity of the performer's affairs. It is not our intention to provide a guide to bookkeeping but we have summarised below the basic records which should be maintained.

(1) A separate bank account should be opened in the performer's business name and all business payments and receipts should be passed through this account. In all cases, it will be necessary to record all receipts and payments of money relating to the business, including particulars of money received for services rendered and money spent on purchases, wages and other items. Details of the amounts received should be analysed in order to show separately the gross income, value added tax and any amount which has been deducted, eg commissions, direct expenses. Control can be exercised over amounts received, particularly in cash form, by the use of pre-numbered receipt books or invoices on which all details can be recorded.

(2) The practice of making disbursements from receipts should be avoided and all cash receipts should be banked intact. Cash disbursements should be made from a separate petty cash float on the basis of properly supported vouchers. This enables the balance on the float to be reconciled with the expenditure incurred.

(3) A record must also be kept of drawings from the business, by way of cash or cheque, to meet private expenditure and also of money put into the business.

(4) If all receipts and payments are tied into the business bank account and cash book, it will be simple to prepare monthly bank reconciliations.

(5) Initially, it will probably be sufficient to account on a cash basis but, where a significant quantity of goods and services are bought or sold on credit, it will become necessary to keep records of creditors and debtors to arrive at the true figure of profit earned in the accounting period and to prepare the trading and profit and loss accounts. Additionally, this information will assist in ensuring that all income is received by providing a record of who owes money.

(6) Any information received from third parties, eg management statements, royalty statements etc, should be compared with the performer's own records and any discrepancies investigated.

1 TMA 1970 ss 86, 88, 93, 95.

(7) Where a decision is taken to utilise a company, the provisions of the Companies Act 1985 regarding accounting records must be considered. These provide, inter alia, that the accounting records must:
   (a) disclose with reasonable accuracy at any time the financial position of the company;
   (b) enable the directors to ensure that any balance sheet or profit and loss account prepared by them gives a true and fair view of the company's state of affairs and profit or loss.

(8) A number of detailed requirements are laid down which, in most cases, will be met by keeping the records referred to above. Annually, in accordance with the Companies Acts, all limited companies must prepare accounts which must be audited. It is proposed that there will be no requirements for accounts to be audited for companies with turnovers of less than £90,000. For companies with turnover between £90,000 and £350,000 the audit requirement will be replaced with a compilation report. There is no statutory requirement for the accounts of sole traders or partnerships to be audited.

(9) Audited accounts must be filed annually with the Registrar of Companies and are available for public inspection (the disclosure requirements are less extensive for small companies).

## Determination of income

Most performers' earnings will result from contracts providing for the exploitation of the performer's services or 'product'. The sources of income cover the whole spectrum from cash, consideration provided in kind in return for services, through to prizes in the form of mementoes and trophies for permanent retention which would not ordinarily be regarded as income subject to taxation. Details of all such income should be recorded. Some of the most common sources of income are as follows.

### Income directly related to performance, whether employed or self-employed

- cash earnings including bonuses;
- payments for the use of copyright;
- benefits-in-kind;
- competition prizes (both in cash and in kind);
- income from exhibition matches/competitions;
- appearance money;
- a share of profits from the exploitation of particular products;
- in the case of some team sports, sportsmen may share in a pool of money or consideration in kind earned by the team members which is then shared out.

### Income from sponsorship and endorsements

For maximum returns, this activity should be compatible with the performer's image which he is trying to project and generally be right for the individual. A great deal of thought often goes into organising the right type of sponsorship deal. Sponsorship agreements can relate to particular products, locations, individuals, groups or teams. Further, the consideration can either be in the form of cash or cash and equipment/products. Additionally, there is often a basic sponsorship sum which is increased by way of bonuses for successful performance. Many top sportsmen derive substantial sums each year from sponsorship by companies involved in sportswear, sports equipment, leisurewear or commercial products generally.

## Promotions and personal appearances

Performers derive income from this activity which is also used to build up their image as personalities. The appearances can include interviews on television, radio and in the press, appearing in light entertainment programmes in the media, opening retail stores, prize givings, social functions and participating in sports days organised by commercial companies for their customers.

## Income from writing

The more successful performer can obtain a useful source of income from articles for magazines and newspapers and autobiographies, although frequently these are 'ghosted'.

## Prizes, unsolicited payments and other 'one-offs'

Often there is scope for tax planning, since the income from these sources tends to be substantial and non-recurring. Benefits and testimonials for sportsmen involved in certain sports provide a possible opportunity for substantial sums to be provided to the sportsman on a tax-free basis. It may be possible to provide lump sum, ex gratia or compensation payments to sportsmen in employment on a tax-free basis when they retire.[2] Signing-on fees are paid in certain sports and there are a whole line of cases dealing with amateurs who have received tax-free sums on giving up their amateur status to turn professional.[3] Finally, prizes are often awarded to sportsmen for particularly meritorious performances, for example, a hole in one in a golf competition or scoring the most goals in a football season. Since the sums can be substantial, close consideration of the tax position is often worthwhile.

## Income for the amateur

Special considerations arise in the case of those sportsmen, who in order to compete under the sport's governing body's rules, must be amateurs. In these cases, it is essential to study these rules closely. These may very

[2] TA 1988 s 188.
[3] *Jarrold v Boustead* (1964) 41 TC 701, CA.

well determine the way in which income from the above sources can be earned and invested. For example, athletics has organised trust funds for athletes which protect their amateur status and allow them to compete internationally.

Generally, it is worth looking at whether this category of sportsmen qualifies for grants. One of the best known grant aiding bodies is the Sports Aid Foundation (SAF) which makes grants to athletes, which are approved by his or her governing body. These are intended to cover out-of-pocket expenses for preparation and training and include such things as travel, subsistence and coaching costs. A new class of elite grant has recently been introduced funded out of money provided by the Foundation for Sport and the Arts. Grants are monitored and the athlete's other sources of income are taken into account. For the more successful, this may mean that the grant will cease if the financial need ceases.

Other grants for training and competition expenses may be available and these are generally negotiated and paid through the amateur sport's governing body. SAF grants are not subject to VAT but are likely to reduce the expenses which the sportsman can deduct for tax purposes.

Grants are also available to many entertainers from arts bodies and these can be of assistance to the artiste in the early stages of his career.

## Contractual arrangements

Clearly, the terms of any contracts to which the performer is a party will have a fundamental impact upon his earnings and, equally importantly, when he is entitled to receive them. However, on occasion, contracts are poorly constructed, badly worded and either silent or vague as to the basis for determining royalty entitlement or share of profits. Many of the difficulties arise from the diverse means which exist for the exploitation of the performer, requiring the contract to be widely drawn. In the case of some sports e.g football, the governing body will specify the form and minimum contents of such contracts.

Proper advice should be taken from a professional adviser with experience in the industry before any contract or agreement is signed to ensure that all clauses and their implications are fully understood. In particular, there are certain specific points which should be expressly defined in the contract or agreement, since they will affect income. These include:

(1) the particular product, services or rights to be exploited;
(2) the length of the contract and how it is to be terminated;
(3) how the products are to be disposed of after the termination of the contract;
(4) who will be entitled to income arising after the contract expires but derived from activities carried out during the contract period;
(5) the territories in which the product or services are to be exploited;
(6) the basis upon which royalties or profit share are to be calculated;
(7) the rate of royalty or percentage share of profits;
(8) the exchange rates to be used for foreign earnings;
(9) the nature of advances made, how they are to be recouped and whether any unrecouped balance is repayable;

(10) the responsibility of each party for various costs, eg travelling expenses, recording costs, location expenses, supporting acts, promotional costs and professional fees;
(11) the requirement to account to the performer for royalties earned within a fixed period of their arising, eg 90 days after the end of each calendar period;
(12) terms such as net and gross should be properly defined;
(13) the rate of any management commission and its basis, eg royalties less production costs, or fees received less first class cost of travel to the relevant venue;
(14) the right to an audit of the underlying records of income on which the performer's earnings are paid;
(15) the treatment of withholding tax;
(16) terms shall be properly defined and expressions such as 'as commonly understood in the industry' etc should be avoided;
(17) whether the sums specified in the contract are exclusive or inclusive of VAT;
(18) whether any signing on fee is payable.

A particular area where many problems of interpretation arise is in the definition of the basis upon which royalties are calculated or profit is shared. Two forms of product exploitation demonstrate the inherent difficulties:

*Example*

A sportsman agrees to allow his name to be used to endorse sports equipment and is to receive an advance plus a royalty of 5% of retail price of the products sold. A number of questions need to be considered:

(1) Does the advance have to be repaid if the necessary sales are not made?
(2) Is the measure of merchandise sold before or after returns to the manufacturer?
(3) Is the manufacturer entitled to make a provision for returns in computing the royalty paid?
(4) How is retail price to be determined – before or after VAT, will it be based on actual returns of sales made by retailers or some sample basis?
(5) What is to happen about surplus stock sold cheaply?

*Example*

A performer agrees to appear at a venue for 20% of the net profits. Clearly the contract needs to define what expenses are to be deducted in computing net profits. It also needs to cover matters such as the quantity of complimentary tickets allowed, the control over ticket sales and receipts. The performer should consider making some form of independent verification of attendees to check the returns he receives from the venue owner or promoter.

All of the above should serve to highlight the crucial importance of having an entitlement to income determined by a precise contract. Areas open to interpretation will require subsequent mutual agreement between the parties or, if this cannot be reached, costly legal action may be necessary.

Consideration also needs to be given to the contractual arrangements within groups. Unfortunately, groups are unlikely to stay together indefinitely and therefore consideration should be given to practical issues at an early stage. These would include:

(1) ownership of the group's name;
(2) ownership of assets eg instruments, vehicles etc;
(3) how income will be split – whether it is different for recording royalties and publishing royalties;
(4) what happens if a member leaves;
(5) whether group members can only perform with the group;
(6) who can contract on behalf of the group;
(7) who controls the group's finances and how much is to be paid out.

These types of issues should be dealt with at an early stage and evidenced in writing.

## Accounting for income

Once an entitlement to income has been determined, the major importance of proper accounting records is to ensure that all income has been recognised and properly computed by the contractual due dates. This objective can only be achieved if the records are sufficiently detailed, accurately kept and updated on a timely basis. There is no reason why such records cannot be maintained as the day-to-day recording of income is normally straightforward. The problems usually only arise in the preparation of financial statements from these basic accounting records and this is the point where professional advice is invaluable.

The Inland Revenue will, in some circumstances, accept 'cash accounts' (see p 22) showing cash receipts and payments but will often require financial statements to be drawn up using generally accepted accounting policies. These policies will determine the period in which income and expenditure are recognised and the basis on which assets and liabilities are valued. The Inland Revenue will also want to ensure that these policies are applied consistently each year and are not changed to suit an individual year's results. Examples of areas for consideration are:

(1) Advances – is the advance treated as income upon receipt or are the related royalties recognised as they are earned?
(2) In which period should income be recognised?
(3) To which period do certain expenses relate, eg publishing advances, recording costs, returns?
(4) The contract year for commercial arrangements, eg sponsorship, where this does not coincide with the performer's financial year.

The benefits of being able to account for income properly are wider than just ensuring that the correct taxable income is assessed:

(1) with proper information available, completeness of income tests may be performed and omissions pursued;
(2) the comparison of actual receipts with contractual entitlement may identify errors and omissions from royalty sources;
(3) the performer will have enough information to enable him to decide whether the right to a royalty audit should be exercised.

## Accounting for expenditure

The control of expenditure is as important to the performer as the control of his income and is far easier to exercise. However, it is the lack of control and the subsequent cash flow problems which have led to the well reported, often spectacular, crises that have befallen performers over the years.

As for income, the accounting records should be maintained on a timely basis, enabling the cash flow to be monitored and problems to be anticipated. This is the most important aspect of accounting for expenditure and, therefore, the system that is set up should be able to cope with the following:

(1) identification of, and distinction between, expenditure relating to the business and that which is personal to the performer;
(2) advances made to staff or others of salary or expenses and how they are to be recovered or set off;
(3) the cost of the performer's equipment and its location;
(4) the cost of contracted assistants such as editors, session musicians, trainers, sound and lighting technicians and their ancillary expenses;
(5) VAT responsibilities.

## Benefits of accounting information

The need to keep accounting records and some of the problems that this entails have now been discussed. However, the benefits may be recognised in a number of ways other than just in terms of computing correct tax liabilities:

(1) Future tax planning can only be carried out if information on current profitability, and therefore estimates of future profitability, are available. For example, in many cases tax savings may be achieved if a period of high earnings can be foreseen and circumstances altered to take that income out of assessment to tax or defer its assessment.
(2) In terms of business planning, it is generally accepted that a proper strategy for commercial development needs up-to-date accounting information on which to base forecasts. No professional adviser will wish to operate with inadequate data. Further, a comparison with forecasts is an important facet of performance measurement.

Clearly, the availability of accounting information is only a tool in the control of personal affairs of a performer or his company but a highly necessary tool if maximum benefits are to be derived from current and future income.

## Information required for the planning process

Accurate financial details are essential to the planning process which should only commence after sufficient information has been obtained from the performer to provide a clear picture of his current financial position, future plans and objectives. This information can be conveniently collected under the following heads:

- personal details (age, marital status, children etc);
- objectives (eg provision for wife, children, maximise current spendable income or capital growth to provide for retirement);
- annual income (earned and unearned, distinguishing different sources);
- annual expenditure (eg housing, living, life assurance, pensions, deeds of covenant, maintenance payments);
- retirement provision (desired retirement age and salary, details of existing arrangements);
- life, health disability and mortgage protection policies;
- gifts (those made in the last seven years);
- wills;
- trusts;
- assets and investments (including estimated market values);
- liabilities;
- investment temperament (eg risk averse or speculative, desired mix of investment portfolio);
- future plans and expectations (eg possible inheritances, proposed gifts, plans to move abroad);
- other professional advisers (eg bank, solicitor, brokers);
- other relevant information.

This information will portray the performer's personal and financial profile and could usefully include a personal cash flow statement as shown in Appendix II. The effect of any action taken as a result of the planning process can then be measured in financial terms.

## Planning considerations

Performers do not have the steady career path applicable to many other occupations. The pattern of earnings is likely to be both unpredictable and uneven being determined to a large extent by public demand and, in the case of sportsmen, success on the field of play.

When planning the affairs of a performer one must bear this in mind, taking into account those elements which are likely to be recurring as well as allowing for contingencies both upward and downward. It is also important to consider the performer's own personal objectives and preferences as there is little point in suggesting that tax can be saved by spending a 365-day period outside the UK (see p 81) if the performer is devoted to his home and family.[4] Some performers' objectives may be geared to the production of the maximum amount of income for personal spending while others are content to live more conservative lives while accumulating capital for the future. Any attempt to force the performer into a rigid pattern is likely to be met with resentment which does not lead to a sound professional relationship although the performer may need counselling on his financial commitments to ensure that his objectives are sensible in the context of his personal circumstances.

An area which needs particular attention is where a group of individuals are concerned as invariably they will have different preferences and objectives. In this regard, it may be preferable to structure arrangements as a joint venture rather than as a partnership, if at all possible, to avoid the prospect of joint and several liability. Furthermore, where incorporation is attractive for whatever reason, the temptation to use a single company to cover all of the individuals' activities should generally be resisted because of the inflexibility which this introduces. It is important that where companies have more than one shareholder there is a comprehensive shareholders' agreement covering what is to happen if there are disputes between them. Obviously where such a collection of individuals is concerned third parties will generally wish to contract with them as a single unit and it may therefore be necessary to incorporate a further company to act as a co-ordinating body, eg each individual performer could have his own service company which is contracted to a single co-ordinating company which has the power to negotiate on his or her behalf.

Consideration must be given to taking out adequate insurance to protect the performer if he is ill or injured and as a consequence unable to perform. The cover will vary from protection for specific events to longer-term cover for loss of earnings. Some types of performer, eg musicians, may need to arrange for public liability insurance.

The planning process should ensure that adequate amounts are set aside for the performer's retirement after the end of his active career. This will normally include pension provision (see Chapter 4) and consideration of investment strategy.

## Investment strategy

Income planning should consider carefully the use of tax effective investments. Basic investment criteria should not, however, be overlooked.

Investments should be selected through an orderly process that deals with the risks as well as returns. The investment plans should be based on personal circumstances and the following factors when establishing a strategy:

(1) personal requirements and preferences;
(2) the lifetime scale of the investment and its liquidity;
(3) the level of acceptable risk;
(4) return on investment;

[4] TA 1988 s 193.

(5) relative risk and return;
(6) diversification.

Tax should be considered in detail, the principal tax factors being:

(1) For income –
  (a) when income is to be received and whether it is to be received gross or after tax;
  (b) whether income tax withheld from the income can, if necessary, be recovered;
  (c) whether bonuses attract full taxation;
  (d) the availability of credit relief for advance corporation tax and overseas tax.
(2) For gains –
  (a) whether the gains are tax exempt or subject to special treatment;
  (b) whether exemption limits apply;
  (c) the cost base of the asset for capital gains tax purposes, eg the availability of March 1982 rebasing and indexation.

For both types of taxable profit timing will be important; not only what tax is payable but when it is payable should be taken into account in the investment strategy.

Appendix III lists basic tax-favoured investments and comments on the tax advantages. It should be noted that neither the listing nor the commentary is exhaustive.

It is important to liaise with other advisers in the financial planning process, eg accountants, solicitors and managers, in order that a joint review can be made of any arrangements. Historical information and projections need to be prepared based on reliable sources of information. It is for this reason we will close this chapter with the emphasis yet again on the need to maintain proper records of the performer's activities.

# 2 Self-employed performers

## Basic rule – employed or self-employed

Self-employed performers are taxed in quite a different way from employed performers. In the absence of evidence to the contrary, it is usual for performers to be taxed as self-employed individuals under Schedule D. Until the last few years it was generally accepted that most performers were self-employed. However, the Inland Revenue attitude has changed and there are increasing attempts to categorise short-term engagements by many performers as employments requiring the employer to operate PAYE and denying relief to individuals for many expenses as not satisfying the strict criteria necessary for Schedule E (see p 58). At the end of 1989 the Inland Revenue announced that it was of the view that actors engaged under standard Equity contracts should properly be regarded as employees. Those actors who could show that they had been assessed under Schedule D for 1986/87, 1987/88 and 1988/89 and satisfied certain other conditions would be allowed to continue to be taxed under Schedule D by having 'reserved Schedule D' status so long as they continued to meet their tax obligations satisfactorily and continued their professional activities without a break. For these purposes a break means a cessation agreed under the Schedule D rules but does not include period of unemployment or of temporary non-theatrical engagements.[1]

This interpretation by the Inland Revenue followed their earlier attacks on those engaged in the film industry and musicians working in orchestras and clubs.

However, the Inland Revenue view was challenged in the case *Hall v Lorimer*[2] where the taxpayer, a self-employed vision mixer, successfully maintained in front of the Special Commissioners, whose decision was upheld in the High Court and the Court of Appeal, that he was properly assessable under Schedule D and not Schedule E. The decision of Nolan L J provides a summary of earlier decisions and concludes that the Special Commissioners were justified in reaching their decision on the facts of the case. While the case may be helpful in resisting Inland Revenue attempts to categorise individuals as employees it should not be relied upon in circumstances where the facts are not closely replicated, ie:

(1) The engagement consisted of numerous short-term engagements of one to two days.
(2) The individual had a professional skill.

1 ESC A75.
2 *Hall v Lorimer* [1994] STC 23, CA.

(3) The individual was registered for VAT.
(4) The individual invoiced for his services and bore the risk of bad debts.
(5) The individual marketed his services.
(6) There were no formal conditions of engagement.
(7) The individual had substantial costs of running his business.

A further attack on the Inland Revenue position was made when the Special Commissioners held in the summer of 1993 that two actors with performers' contracts with theatres were self-employed. The Commissioners considered that the contracts in question were similar to those for radio, television and film contracts and were not employments but instead engagements in the course of a Schedule D self-employment. They also considered other circumstances which lead to a conclusion of self-employment - engagements frequently overlap, actors have their own business agent and they do not become part and parcel of the theatre. Interestingly the Commissioners said there were no anomalies in the older cases of *Davies v Braithwaite*,[3] where an actress undertaking a series of engagements was held to be self-employed and *Fall v Hitchen*[4] where a dancer was held to be an employee of an opera company. The distinction appears to be that general theatre work can be regarded as Schedule D while repertory work is Schedule E. The Inland Revenue, however, have stated that they do not regard the case as a test case.

As a general rule most sportsmen participating in team sports are likely to be regarded as employees in view of the element of control which is required of the sportsman by the team club. However, even employed sportsmen may have self-employed activities outside their employment with a particular club; in such cases, particularly for the successful performer, their tax affairs are likely to be complex. Self-employed status is more likely to be found in those sports where the sportsman participates on an individual basis although even here he may be employed by his own service company provided he is allowed to do so under the rules of the sport's governing body.

## Amateur status

In many sports sportsmen are not allowed to compete if they earn income by competing, teaching, training or coaching in that sport. They are, however, usually allowed to be paid expenses, either by way of direct reimbursement of their out-of-pocket expenses from competing or by daily allowances which are designed to cover other out-of-pocket costs or payments towards training expenses.

Amateur status for the purposes of a particular sports body's rules and regulations is not automatically accepted by the Inland Revenue as taking the sportsman outside the tax net. The principal reasons for this are that, firstly, he may actually receive taxable income in breach of his particular sports body's rules or, alternatively, even if the income is received within the body's rules it may be held centrally by the governing body in trust

[3] *Davies v Braithwaite* (1933) 18 TC 198, KB.
[4] *Fall v Hitchin* [1973] STC 66, Ch D.

on his behalf and remain taxable. In this latter event it may be paid out either on the individual's voluntary retirement or on enforced retirement because of illness, injury or death. Where individual sportsmen become financially successful it may be possible for them to establish an individual trust fund, although again they are usually only permitted to use the accumulated funds against expenses incurred in carrying on their sporting activities. In these circumstances the Inland Revenue is likely to regard the income as taxable currently, and indeed the various funds which have been established for the benefit of athletes are regarded by the Inland Revenue as taxable currently, since they are effectively held by the governing body or trustees on bare trust for the benefit of the athlete. The second reason why taxable income may arise for the amateur is that the expenses which the governing body allows him to draw are not necessarily tax deductible. Just because a particular sport's rules allow these payments to be made whilst not contravening his amateur status it does not follow that the Inland Revenue will necessarily regard them as tax deductible. It is for these sorts of reasons that the amateur's participation in his sport may give rise to financial gain, whether allowed by the governing body or not, resulting in tax reporting requirements and tax liabilities. This may arise currently if full disclosure is made to the Inland Revenue, or later when the Inland Revenue catch up with the sportsman, following which penalties and interest will also usually be imposed.

The Inland Revenue will normally look to the existence of any contractual obligation for services in return for payments made. If such obligations exist it is likely to argue that the payments are taxable. Thus, the Inland Revenue regards contract players involved in 'semi-professional' football as having an employment relationship with their club.

The irrelevance of 'amateur' status for tax purposes was recently emphasised by an Inland Revenue challenge on referees and officials within football. Special Office argued initially that they were employees of the organising bodies but later conceded self-employed status following a decision to that effect for national insurance purposes.

## For the love of the game

It may be possible for sportsmen to be treated as participating in their particular sport 'for the love of the game' although this is likely to apply only in the initial stages of their careers. In this case there may be no taxable income arising in relation to payments of expenses. The Inland Revenue has agreed since 1982 with such treatment in the case of non-contract players involved in Association Football in England. The Inland Revenue did not contest this position, which was adopted on behalf of such non-contract players, where the individual only received specific reimbursement of actual travelling and other out-of-pocket expenses. This included the cost of travelling from home to the ground and the training ground. The Inland Revenue Special Office in the past accepted that, in effect, non-contract players within this category were not employees and were, therefore, outside the scope of the PAYE regulations. It was also acceptable for clubs to reimburse legitimate travelling expenses by car incurred by non-contract players on any reasonable basis which did not exceed the current Automobile Association rate of an average family saloon. Furthermore, such players could also be reimbursed sums laid out on necessary equipment such as football boots, training gear and other out-of-pocket costs without giving rise to tax liabilities.

Where, however, an individual received more than reimbursement of specific travelling and other out-of-pocket costs, eg appearance money, was received in addition, he is regarded as an employee and taxable on the total sums received subject to a deduction of those expenses incurred wholly, exclusively and necessarily in the performance of his employment duties. Such expenses would not of course include travelling costs from home to the ground. An individual receiving a round sum expense allowance in excess of his actual expenditure would also be treated as an employee but many non-contract players found that, since they were travelling substantial distances to play and train for their chosen club, the round sum expense allowances which they received did not fully cover their out-of-pocket costs computed on the above basis. In many cases, however, the proper accounting and reimbursement procedures have not been adhered to resulting in problems for the clubs and the players.

The Inland Revenue have been reviewing the operation of PAYE in semi-professional clubs and are unhappy with the reimbursement procedures operated by many clubs. As a consequence many non-contract players may find themselves within the tax net in relation to 'expenses' payments and would be well advised to confirm the position with their club.

## Casual earnings

If an individual receives occasional earnings from activities such as writing articles for magazines, he will normally be assessed under Schedule D, Case VI rather than Schedule D, Case II.[5] Sportsmen may sometimes be provided with equipment or kit and where this is unsolicited it may escape tax. Where, however, future supplies or payments depend upon the future use of the supplier's product this will constitute taxable income. The effect of this is that the income will be assessed to tax in the year it is actually received[6] rather than on the basis detailed below. Additionally, any loss which may be made can only be set off against Schedule D, Case VI income of the same year or of future years,[7] rather than against general income, as is the case with Schedule D, Cases I and II.[8]

Many sporting personalities do, however, organise their activities off the field sufficiently to establish the existence of a trade or profession. Sometimes income can arise from this source in addition to an employment which the sportsman has with the sports club or organisation. In other cases it may be part of his self-employed activity.

## Earnings/cash basis

Under Schedule D, it is normal for a performer to be taxed on the income earned in a particular basis period irrespective of when the cash is received.

5 TA 1988 s 18.
6 Ibid s 69.
7 Ibid s 392.
8 Ibid ss 380, 381.

However, in certain circumstances, the Inland Revenue will accept the cash (or 'conventional') basis of assessment, with tax being assessed on the basis of the cash income received, debtors and creditors being ignored. The cash basis cannot be used for the first three accounting years of the profession.

If a performer is on a cash basis of accounting, it is possible for him to switch to an earnings basis, but in order for him to do so he has to bring into account unpaid bills and work in progress at the date of change. This could result in a substantial additional charge to tax.[9]

## Assessment of income

Currently the normal basis of assessment of tax for self-employed persons, including performers, is the 'preceding year' basis.[10] As will be seen, this basis of assessment can provide significant cash flow advantages and in certain circumstances significant amounts of profits can escape a charge to tax. However, for individuals commencing their trade or profession after 5 April 1994 new rules will apply. For all performers new rules will also apply for 1997/98 and onwards.

On the current basis, the amount assessed for a tax year is calculated on the tax-adjusted profits for the accounting year ended within the preceding tax year.

*Example*

| *Accounting period* | *Income tax year of assessment* |
|---|---|
| Year ended 30 April 1991 (ie ends in 1991/92) | 1992/93 |
| Year ended 30 April 1992 (ie ends in 1992/93) | 1993/94 |
| Year ended 30 April 1993 (ie ends in 1993/94) | 1994/95 |

## Opening and closing years under current rules

A new business has no preceding year, so there are special provisions covering the periods when a performer commences to exercise his profession.[11] There are also special provisions to cover the years immediately preceding the cessation of a profession.[12]

### Opening years

In many cases, it may be difficult to establish when a performer actually commences his profession, particularly where he may have previously carried it on as a hobby. It may eventually be a matter of negotiation with the Inland Revenue as to the actual date which is to be regarded as the commencement date. Sometimes arguing for an early commencement date

9 TA 1988 s 103(2)(b).
10 Ibid s 60(1) (prior to amendment by FA 1994).
11 Ibid ss 61, 62 (prior to amendment by FA 1994).
12 Ibid s 63 (prior to amendment by FA 1994).

may suit the performer (see p 26) but if relief is sought for losses the Inland Revenue may challenge this.

| *Year of assessment* | *Profits used as a basis for assessment* |
|---|---|
| First | 'Actual' profits from date of commencement to the following 5 April, taking a proportion of a longer accounting period, if necessary. |
| Second | Actual profits for the first 12 months of trading, made up by apportionment, if necessary. (Part or all of these profits may have formed the basis of the assessed profit in the first tax year.) |
| Third | Normal preceding year basis, ie profits of the 12-month accounting period ending in the preceding year of assessment (if no year fits this description, the assessment is normally based again on the profits of the first 12 months of trading, although this is at the discretion of the Inland Revenue). |

In all these cases, where the period for which accounts have been made up does not coincide with the tax assessment periods, it is necessary to apportion profits on a time basis to the appropriate period in order to arrive at a figure of assessable profit.

## *Example*

A performer commences his profession on 1 September 1988 and makes up accounts to 30 April in each year with the following results:

| *Period* | *Income* |
|---|---|
| | £ |
| 8 months to 30 April 1989 | 1,500 |
| 12 months to 30 April 1990 | 2,000 |
| 12 months to 30 April 1991 | 3,000 |

| *Year of assessment* | *Basis period* | | *Assessable income* |
|---|---|---|---|
| | | £ | £ |
| 1988/89 | 7 months to 5 April 1989 | | |
| | $\frac{7}{8} \times$ £1,500 | | 1,312 |
| 1989/90 | First 12 months to 31 August 1989 | | |
| | ie 8 months to 30 April 1989 | 1,500 | |
| | plus $\frac{4}{12} \times$ £2,000 | 666 | |
| | | | 2,166 |
| 1990/91 | No 12-month accounting period ends in 1989/90 so 1990/91 is first 12 months again | | 2,166 |
| 1991/92 | Normal preceding year basis, 12 months to 30 April 1990 | | 2,000 |

This approach can give rise to anomalies because of the double taxation of certain profits, and it is possible to elect to be taxed on the actual profits arising in the first three years if this is beneficial.[13]

### *Example*

Same accounting periods as above, with the following results:

| *Period* | *Income* |
|---|---|
| | £ |
| 8 months to 30 April 1989 | 9,000 |
| 12 months to 30 April 1990 | 10,000 |
| 12 months to 30 April 1991 | 9,000 |

| | | | *Normal basis* | *Elective basis* |
|---|---|---|---|---|
| | | £ | £ | £ |
| 1988/89 | 7 months to 5 April 1989 7/8 × £9,000 | | 7,875 | 7,875 |
| 1989/90 | First 12 months to 30 September 1989 ie 8 months to 30 April 1989 | 9,000 | | |
| | plus 4/12 × £10,000 | 3,333 | | |
| | | | 12,333 | |
| | Actual profits for year to 5 April 1990 ie 1/8 × £9,000 | 1,125 | | |
| | plus 11/12 × £10,000 | 9,167 | | |
| | | | | 10,292 |
| 1990/91 | First 12 months again | | 12,333 | |
| | Actual profits for year to 5 April 1991 ie 1/12 × £10,000 plus | 833 | | |
| | 11/12 × £9,000 | 8,250 | | |
| | | | | 9,083 |
| 1991/92 | Normal preceding-year basis 12 months to 30 April 1990 | | 10,000 | 10,000 |
| Total assessable profits | | | £42,541 | £37,250 |
| Reduction in assessable profits if election made | | | £5,291 | |

Before any election is made, it will be necessary to examine the marginal rate of tax for the years in question to ensure that there is in fact a tax saving. In the example this is not important as the elective basis gives lower assessable profits for both 1989/90 and 1990/91. Assuming a constant tax rate of 25% there is a tax saving (on the above figures) of £1,322.75.

[13] TA 1988 s 62(2) (prior to amendment by FA 1994).

It will be noted that, in the opening years, the results of certain periods form the basis of assessment for more than one tax year and this does provide some scope for tax planning by minimising profits for those periods. In particular, it is important to review the performer's activities to ensure that the earliest possible commencement date is used. If this can include periods when income was low, eg when a musician is playing for low fees in pubs, etc before a recording contract is signed, this will generally result in minimal profits being 'doubly assessed' and also means that the preceding year basis, with its cash flow advantages, is available when significant earnings are being made.

## Closing years

The provisions can be summarised as follows:

| Year of assessment | Profit used as basis period for assessment |
|---|---|
| Last but two | Preceding year basis |
| Last but one | Preceding year basis |
| Last | Actual profits from 6 April to date of cessation |

As a corollary to the taxpayer's option mentioned above for the 'actual' basis in the second and third years of assessment, the Inland Revenue has the power to review the assessment for the last but two and last but one years of assessment (but not one only of those years) to 'actual' if this gives a higher total assessment than the 'preceding year' basis.[14]

It should be appreciated that, even if the Inland Revenue exercises its right to re-open the penultimate and pre-penultimate years, some income will inevitably fall out of charge to tax, because of the way the closing rules operate, and this can give rise to considerable tax savings.

### *Example*

A performer ceases to exercise his profession on 31 May 1992. His tax-adjusted profits for the periods to cessation are as follows:

| | £ |
|---|---|
| 12 months to 30 April 1989 | 40,000 |
| 12 months to 30 April 1990 | 45,000 |
| 12 months to 30 April 1991 | 50,000 |
| 13 months to 31 May 1992 | 75,000 |
| | £210,000 |

[14] TA 1988 s 63(1)(b) (prior to amendment by FA 1994).

| *Tax year* | | | *Normal basis* | *Revenue option* |
|---|---|---|---|---|
| | | £ | £ | £ |
| 1992/93 | $\frac{2}{13}$ × £75,000 | | 11,538 | 11,538 |
| 1991/92 | Year to 30 April 1990 | | 45,000 | |
| | Revenue option: actual profits for 1991/92 | | | |
| | $\frac{11}{13}$ × £75,000 | 63,462 | | |
| | $\frac{1}{12}$ × £50,000 | 4,167 | | |
| | | | | 67,629 |
| 1990/91 | Year to 30 April 1989 | | 40,000 | |
| | Revenue option: actual profits for 1990/91 | | | |
| | $\frac{11}{12}$ × £50,000 | 45,833 | | |
| | $\frac{1}{12}$ × £45,000 | 3,750 | | |
| | | | | 49,583 |
| | | | £96,538 | £128,750 |

Even with the exercise of the Inland Revenue's option, profits of £81,250 (£210,000 – £128,750) fall out of charge to tax. At a 40% marginal rate of tax, this represents a tax saving of £32,500.

It should be noted that the opening and closing year rules outlined above apply not only when a performer commences and ceases the exercise of his profession, but also when:

(1) he introduces a partner; or
(2) the business is transferred to a company.[15]

It is possible, on the introduction of a partner, to elect to treat the business as continuing and therefore avoid the commencement and cessation provisions if so desired.[16]

These provisions currently allow considerable scope for tax planning in the situations set out above.

## The new rules for the taxation of the self-employed

New tax rules for the self-employed have now been set out in the Finance Act 1994. Generally speaking they apply with effect from 6 April 1997. Transitional provisions apply in 1996/97.

Businesses set up and commenced after 5 April 1994 will be subject to the new rules from the outset. On the other hand, existing businesses which cease before 5 April 1997 will not be affected by the new rules. Nor will a business which ceases before 5 April 1998 providing the Inland Revenue so directs.

[15] TA 1988 s 113.
[16] Ibid s 113(2) (prior to amendment by FA 1994).

## Current year basis

Profits for the 12 months ending on the accounting date falling within a tax year will form the basis for the tax assessment for that year.[17]

*Example*

X makes up accounts to 30 April. Y makes up accounts to 31 March.

In 1997/98, X will be assessed on profits for the year to 30 April 1997. Y will be assessed on profits for the year to 31 March 1998.

## Commencement rules

As currently, the chargeable profits of a new business in its first tax year are based on the actual amount arising between commencement and the following 5 April.[18]

For the second year, the business will be assessed on the 12 months to its current accounting date. If that is less than a 12-month period, tax will be based on the first 12 months' profit.[19]

*Example*

X and Y started trading on 1 November 1994. X makes up accounts to 30 April. Y makes up accounts to 31 March.

Since the business started after 5 April 1994, the new rules apply. For 1994/95, the basis period would be 1 November 1994 to 5 April 1995 for both individuals.

In 1995/96, the basis periods are:

for X – 1 November 1994 to 30 October 1995 (first 12 months)
for Y – 12 months to 31 March 1996

In 1996/97, both firms will be on a normal current year basis (see example above)

For X, in this example, there is a 6-month period from 1 November 1994 to 5 April 1995 which is taxed twice, ie forms the basis for tax assessments in 1994/95 and 1995/96. The profit in this period is known as 'overlap profit' and there are provisions for reducing X's future profit by this amount.[20] This would happen either on cessation or on a change of accounting date (see examples below).

17 TA 1988 s 60.
18 Ibid s 61(1).
19 Ibid s 61(2).
20 Ibid s 63A.

*Example*

X's profit in the period 1 November 1994 to 30 October 1995 is £600,000. The assessments will be:

| *Tax year* | *Based on* | *Assessment* |
|---|---|---|
| | | £ |
| 1994/95 | 1 November 1994 to 5 April 1995 | 250,000 |
| 1995/96 | 1 November 1994 to 30 October 1995 | 600,000 |
| | | £850,000 |

The 'overlap profit' is therefore £250,000.

## Cessation rules

The final tax year will now be based on the profit from the end of the year of account in the previous tax year to the date of cessation.[1]

*Example*

If X and Y both cease on 30 June 1998, the final assessments for 1998/99 will be based on the following periods:

for X – 15 months from 1 May 1997 to 30 June 1998
for Y – 3 months from 1 April 1998 to 30 June 1998

There will be a deduction from the final assessable profit of X in respect of the 6 months overlap profit mentioned above.[2]

*Example*

X's final profits in the 15-month period to 30 June 1998 were £750,000. The 1998/99 assessment would be:

| | £ |
|---|---|
| Assessment for basis period | 750,000 |
| Less: 'overlap' profit (example above) | (250,000) |
| | £500,000 |

## Transitional relief

The last year of the preceding year basis for individuals subject to it will be 1995/96. As already mentioned, the new rules will apply from 1997/98. This leaves one transitional year to mop up two years' profits.

1 TA 1988 s 63.
2 Ibid s 63A.

Where there is no change of accounting date the solution adopted is to average the aggregate profits of the intervening years.[3]

### *Example*

X is currently assessed on a preceding year basis in respect of accounts to 30 April.

Tax will be assessed as follows in the relevant years:

| | |
|---|---|
| 1995/96 | profit for the year to 30 April 1994 |
| 1996/97 | one half of the aggregate profit for the 2 years to 30 April 1996 |
| 1997/98 | profit for the year to 30 April 1997 |

## Incorporation

When a performer operating alone or in partnership transfers his business to a company, some relief from the normal cessation rules may be forthcoming. The advantages of using a company are discussed in the next chapter and the main tax and commercial considerations are summarised in Appendix IV. Incorporation can provide a useful tax planning tool with potential benefits arising from a 'drop out' of profits under the closing year rules (see p 26) or from a three-year carry back of terminal losses.

Normally, on the cessation of a business, all assets used in the profession on which capital allowances have been claimed must be valued at market value and a balancing charge (ie market value up to cost less capital allowances not yet claimed) is added to the trading profits for the final period.[4] If market value is less than such allowances a balancing allowance is deducted from the profits. Where, however, there is a balancing charge, it may be possible for an election to be made for the assets to be transferred at tax written-down value.[5] Any balancing adjustment would be deferred until the assets are ultimately disposed of and would be based on the ultimate disposal proceeds.

The relevant legislation provides that this election can be made where the company succeeds to a trade which includes a profession or vocation. However, as a company can only carry on a trade it cannot succeed to the profession carried on by the performer; strictly, therefore, the election cannot be made. The Inland Revenue does not always take this point but it may be preferable to sell the assets to the company for a nominal sum. As the company will use the assets for the purposes of its trade, the Inland Revenue cannot replace this price with market value.

Consideration also needs to be given to other capital assets held by the performer in connection with his business. It is unlikely that he will have goodwill which could be sold but there may be some inherent value in his name or, in the case of an entertainer, the band name, particularly if there are contracts in force at the time exploiting this. Any goodwill

3 FA 1994 Sch 20 para 1.
4 CAA 1990 s 24.
5 Ibid s 77.

can be transferred to the company without incurring capital gains tax either as part of a transfer of the whole business in return for the issue of shares, in which case the base cost of the shares is reduced by the value of the goodwill,[6] or by gifting the goodwill to the newly incorporated company.[7]

The performer may also have rights to continuing income from existing contracts and copyrights. The performer could retain the rights to such income and receive the income as post cessation receipts taxable under Schedule D, Case VI[8] (see p 22). However, if the intention of the incorporation is to engineer a cessation of the performer's profession, then any renegotiation of any of the existing contracts or entering into new arrangements to exploit the retained rights might be regarded as continuing to carry on the profession. It may, therefore, be preferable to transfer the pre-existing rights to the new company. If a value is placed on the rights this would be taxable as a cessation receipt. This charge may be avoided by gifting the rights to the new company; great care is needed and professional advice should always be taken.

### Value added tax

Where a business is transferred as a going concern VAT should not be accounted for on the values of the assets transferred.[9]

### Stamp duty

Stamp duty at the rate of 1% may be payable on the value of assets where they are transferred to a company unless the transfer is made by way of gift. Assets which can be transferred by physical delivery, eg stock, will not be subject to duty but those requiring a document will normally attract duty.

## Payment of tax

Income tax in respect of Schedule D Cases I and II income is currently payable in two equal instalments on 1 January in the year of assessment and on 1 July following the end of that year or (if later) 30 days after the issue of a notice of assessment by the Inspector of Taxes.[10]

The choice of the date to which accounts are drawn up can affect the period between the earning of profits and the payment of the tax attributable to those profits, thereby allowing funds to be employed in the business or elsewhere for a longer period, ie a 'cash flow' advantage.

6 TCGA 1992 s 162.
7 Ibid s 165.
8 TA 1988 s 103.
9 SI 1992/3192 art 5.
10 TA 1988 s 5(2).

*Example*

Accounts drawn up to 31 March 1990 – tax payable on 1 January 1991 and 1 July 1991.
Accounts drawn up to 30 April 1990 – tax payable on 1 January 1992 and 1 July 1993.

A delay of 30 days in the accounting date results in a 12-month delay in the payment of tax.

Following the change in the basis of assessment for the self-employed detailed on p 27 payment dates for taxation will change for 1996/97 and subsequent years. Interim payments on account of the liability for a year of assessment will be made on 31 January in the tax year and 31 July following the year. These would each be equal to half the liability for the previous year or half the estimated liability for the current year if lower. Any balance due would be payable on 31 January following the year of assessment.[11]

Interest, which is not deductible in computing profits for tax purposes, will be charged where tax is paid late.[12] The current rate is 5.5% pa.

## Partnerships

The basis of assessment for partnerships is the same as that for individuals, ie the preceding year basis with special rules for opening and closing years. Special opening and closing year provisions apply on a change in the partnership structure,[13] unless a continuation election is made by all the partners, both before and after the change, within two years after the date of the change.[14] Where no elections are made profits are taxed as follows in the years around the change in partnership:

| *Year of assessment* | *Profit used as basis period for assessment* |
|---|---|
| OLD PARTNERSHIP | |
| Last but two | Preceding year basis |
| Last but one | Preceding year basis |
| Last (year of change) | Actual profits from 6 April to date of partnership change |

The Inland Revenue has the option to revise the assessment for the last but two and last but one years of assessment to 'actual' if it wishes.[15]

11 FA 1994 s 192.
12 TMA 1970 s 86.
13 TA 1988 s 61(4) (prior to amendment by FA 1994).
14 TA 1988 s 113(2).
15 Ibid s 63 (prior to amendment by FA 1994).

NEW PARTNERSHIP

| | |
|---|---|
| First year (year of change) | Actual profits arising following partnership change |
| Second year | Actual profits arising |
| Third year | Actual profits arising |
| Fourth year | Actual profits arising |
| Fifth year | Profits of period of account ending in the preceding fiscal year |
| Sixth year onwards | Profits of period of account ending in the preceding fiscal year |

The taxpayer has the option to be assessed on the actual profits arising in the fifth and sixth years.[16] The election relating to these years must be made within six years of the later of the two years to which the election will apply.

These rules only apply when a partner is added to or deleted from an existing partnership, not to the introduction of a first partner by a sole trader. In this case the opening and closing year rules described on pp 23 to 27 apply.

The payment date for tax due from a partnership is the same as for individuals, ie 1 January in the year of assessment and 1 July following. It should be noted that the tax is assessed on, and is the joint and several liability of, all the partners irrespective of their own allocation of the tax liability among them.[17] The tax assessment is split among the partners in their profit-sharing ratio in the actual tax year of assessment, which can result in incoming partners being liable for tax on income earned by partners who have left where a continuation election has been made.

The changes to the basis of assessment for the self-employed which are described on pp 27 to 30 will also apply to partnerships.

There will be no deemed cessations and commencements of a partnership when there is a partnership change after 5 April 1997. Instead, individual partners will have their share of the partnership's overall taxable profit/allowable loss computed as if they earned their share as a sole trader.[18] Thus incoming and outgoing partners in partnerships with year ends other than 5 April will have a basis of assessment which differs from that of the other partners. An incoming partner will create an overlap profit and an outgoing partner can benefit from a reduction for any past overlap profit.

Additionally, it is also proposed that the joint and several liability of partners for tax on partnership profit would cease and instead each partner would be liable for tax on his share of the profits. Profits would be allocated for tax purposes on the basis used in the partnership accounts rather than the basis applying for the year of assessment.

The use of a partnership as a method of mitigating tax liabilities should not be overlooked. For example, it may be possible to introduce a performer's working wife as a partner thereby significantly reducing the overall tax liability.

16 TA 1988 s 62 (prior to amendment by FA 1994).
17 Ibid s 111 (prior to amendment by FA 1994).
18 Ibid s 111.

*Example*

A performer has assessable income from his profession of £60,000 which, at 1992/93 rates, would be subject to tax as follows:

| | £ | £ |
|---|---|---|
| Professional income | | 60,000 |
| Personal allowance | 3,445 | |
| Married couples allowance | 1,720 | (5,165) |
| Taxable income | | 54,835 |
| Tax thereon (after relief for NIC) | | 18,091 |
| Class 4 NIC thereon | | 941 |
| Total tax and NIC | | £19,032 |

If his wife had been introduced as a working partner, eg manager entitled to a 25% share of profit, the tax would be:

| | | *Husband* | | *Wife* |
|---|---|---|---|---|
| | £ | £ | £ | £ |
| Professional income | | 45,000 | | 15,000 |
| Personal allowance | 3,445 | | 3,445 | |
| Married couples allowance | 1,720 | | - | |
| | | 5,165 | | 3,445 |
| Taxable income | | 39,835 | | 11,555 |
| Tax thereon (after relief for NIC) | | 12,091 | | 2,719 |
| Class 4 NIC thereon | | 941 | | 559 |
| Total tax and NIC | | 13,032 | | 3,278 |
| | | | £16,061 | |

The overall saving is £2,722

## Taxable income

Performers can receive a number of different types of payment, of which the following normally constitute taxable income:

- commissions;
- performance and appearance fees;
- writing fees;
- sponsorship and endorsement income;
- merchandising income;
- amounts received for assignments of copyright (see p 43 for reliefs);
- subsidies towards business expenditure (by reducing the tax deductible expenditure);
- subsidies towards living costs.

## Sponsorship income

Sponsorship arrangements usually provide for the performer to provide services of a promotional nature helping the sport or to sell a product. They can take many forms. Consideration can be in cash or in kind and in the case of a sportsman can sometimes depend on his performance. They are usually evidenced in writing and the income is generally taxable.

What is not always clear in the case of sportsmen is how the income is taxed. The two major alternatives are whether income is from employment or self-employment. In determining this it will be necessary not only to look at the sponsorship agreement but at all the surrounding facts and circumstances. In most cases, however, it is unlikely that an employment relationship will be created although the income may be taxed under Schedule E where the individual is employed, eg by a sports club, and the sponsorship agreement is with his employer. Sometimes part of the sponsorship payments received by the employing club are passed on to the team members. In other situations the employing club may arrange for benefits to be provided by the sponsor to its employed sportsmen, eg the provision of sponsors' cars. Where cash is paid on in this way it will be subject to tax and PAYE should be applied. Where the benefits are provided in kind then a tax liability will arise under the benefits and expenses provisions for higher paid employees.[19] An expense deduction may, however, be available,[20] although the Inland Revenue may challenge a deduction for leisurewear provided under the wholly and exclusively rule.

Where the sponsorship is of a professional sportsman, even though he may be employed, it is likely that the sponsorship income will be treated as coming from a self-employed activity outside his employment. In this event he will be able to take a deduction for those expenses incurred in earning the income. Where consideration is received in kind it is likely that the Inland Revenue will argue that the measure of his 'profit' is the market value of what is received. However, tax relief may be available either as an expense in the case of sportswear or by way of capital allowances if equipment is provided. There may be advantages in the sponsor retaining the ownership of any equipment provided in this way with the sportsman using it free of charge.

## Royalties

Royalty income received by the person who created the copyrighted work counts as trading income. It is useful at this juncture to differentiate between royalties and income for services provided, as certain of the reliefs described later only apply to royalty income.

Royalties only arise where the performer owns at some time the copyright in his product. Accordingly, if under the terms of a contract the finished product belongs to someone else, the performer will, in fact, be receiving consideration for services rendered, ie salary or fees, and not royalty income.

It is not unusual for performers to receive advances on account of their future royalty earnings. The advances will generally be recouped from these

19 TA 1988 Part V Chapter II.
20 Ibid s 198.

royalty earnings. In some cases, the contract may prescribe that any advance unrecovered by a certain date will be repayable by the performer, ie a recoverable royalty.

If the performer's accounts are being prepared on an earnings basis, non-repayable advances will be attributed to the year in which they are receivable. A case can be made for spreading such advances over the term of the agreement or in accordance with the actual earnings pattern. If such a stance is taken it is likely to be challenged by the Inland Revenue which generally regards such advances as taxable in the year when receivable.

Where the accounts are prepared on the cash basis, all advances are attributed to the year of receipt. Any repayment should be deductible in the year it is made.

In the case of recording artists, the advances will often be made to cover the costs of producing the record master. In such circumstances, the full amount of the advance should be recorded as income in accordance with the artist's accepted tax treatment.

### Recording costs

The basis for deduction of the costs in recording an album or single will depend upon the contractual position between the performer and the record company. If the master tape or disc remains the property of the performer and is then licensed or assigned to the record company, the expenditure incurred is capital in nature. However, CAA 1990 s 68 deems the expenditure to be revenue in nature and requires the expenditure to be relieved on a just and reasonable basis over the period income from the master is expected to be realised. In practice, costs are often written off in the year they are incurred but the Inland Revenue may challenge this in the case of well established acts as Statement of Practice SP1/93 only refers to this practice being acceptable where the artist or group is not well known, the costs of productions are relatively small and the predicted life is less than 12 months. It is possible to elect for the costs to be treated as capital expenditure and capital allowances to be claimed (see p 41).

If the performer is merely performing services and title to the master never belongs to him then the expenditure is revenue in nature and should be expensed. Again, in practice the costs are normally written off in the year incurred.

## Non-taxable income

Prizes received by performers are generally non-taxable[1] unless the work was specifically performed with the prize in mind, or if the work was actively solicited. Clearly where sportsmen are competing with a prize in mind such amounts will constitute taxable income, the measure of which will probably be market value in the case of prizes in kind.

1 *Simpson v John Reynolds & Co (Insurances) Ltd* [1975] STC 271, CA; *Moore v Griffiths* (1972) 48 TC 338, Ch D.

For instance, a novelist who wins the Booker prize will not be taxed, as the book will not have been written primarily to win the prize.[2] Where, however, a novelist writes specifically for entry in a competition, any eventual prize will normally be subject to tax as part of the profits of his profession.

Certain Arts Council grants and subsidies may be tax free, but where grants are provided to supplement the artist's professional income, they may be taxable, even if made gratuitously.[3]

Sportsmen sometimes receive substantial sums by way of an inducement to become registered and subsequently employed with a particular sports club or organisation. Such payments are prohibited under the rules of many sports bodies unless they are made in accordance with the body's own particular rules. Accordingly, before reviewing the taxation aspects of such a payment it is always advisable to look at the applicable body's rules. It has been possible to make inducement payments or signing on fees under the rules of two particular sports, rugby league and football, and it is payments within these sports that have commanded the headlines over the years. Historically such payments have often been accorded tax-free status by the courts because of their capital, as opposed to income, nature.[4] Increasingly, the Inland Revenue is seeking to tax such payments although there may still be scope for obtaining tax-free treatment for them where the following guidelines are met:

(1) The sportsman is permanently giving up or losing an advantage as a result of taking up the position, eg amateur status. This could also include the loss of a secure career or the disruption to personal life by moving house/location or a change in present lifestyle.
(2) The payment is non-returnable if the individual does not take up the new position.
(3) The payment is in no way connected with past or future services, nor is it to be spread over the period of the new contract.
(4) The individual's remuneration under the new contract is at full market rates and the value of the advantage which is being given up should be specifically recognised in the negotiating process. If it is merely added as an afterthought when the package has been negotiated, in an attempt to obtain tax-free status, it is unlikely to succeed.
(5) The relevant documentation is available to support the tax-free nature of the payment; often this is absent.

If the capital sum received can be differentiated in this way from the performer's professional income, it may be possible to justify capital treatment. However, capital treatment is generally not available for payments of signing on fees to professional footballers in England. This is because under English Premier and Football League rules signing on fees must be inserted in the player's contract and paid in equal annual instalments over the contract period. Any instalments are forfeited if he is transferred to another club at his own written request. As a result such signing on fees have an income rather than capital character.

It should be noted that a performer in a profession may generally make

[2] Special Commissioners decision.
[3] *Smart v Lincolnshire Sugar Co Ltd* (1937) 20 TC 643, HL.
[4] *Jarrold v Boustead* (1964) 41 TC 701, CA.

a gift of his services or of an unfinished product without being assessed to tax on any notional profit which he has forgone.[5]

A novelist could, for instance, give away the copyright of an unpublished novel without being assessed to income tax on the value of that copyright. He may, however, be subject to capital gains tax and potentially inheritance tax on the value of the asset transferred. Given that the novel is unpublished, it would probably be possible to argue that it had a relatively low value in comparison with the value of the potential royalty flow, and it may be possible for the donor and donee to elect to transfer at nil cost for capital gains tax purposes provided the transfer is not potentially exempt for inheritance tax purposes.[6] Expenses incurred in creating the asset would, however, not be allowable as a deduction against the novelist's professional income. Such planning could be used to transfer a potentially valuable asset into a trust for the benefit of a child of the performer.

A further possibility would be to assign the copyright in works not yet created, so that future copyrights vests in the assignee. It can be argued that the value of unwritten works is low and therefore that the capital gains tax and inheritance tax implications of such an assignment to, say, a child of the performer would be insignificant.

## Return of expenses

Many of the payments receivable by a performer are required to be 'declared' to the Inland Revenue by the payer.[7] The necessary returns are normally made annually, but can be at shorter intervals if this is more convenient, and are in respect of:

(1) payments made to persons (other than employees) providing entertainment etc, whether directly (as in the case of actors, artists and musicians) or indirectly (as in the case of authors, composers, arrangers, designers, producers, promoters and impresarios etc);
(2) all payments in the nature of commission of any kind made to persons other than employees (eg commissions paid to advertising agents);
(3) all payments in respect of copyright.

A copy of the Inland Revenue form 46R-1 used for supplying this information is shown in Appendix V.

Returns need not be made where the total payments do not exceed £250 to any one person or where payments are made under deduction of income tax in which case the appropriate form R185 should be supplied to the payee.

## Expenses

The general rule for self-employed performers is that, for expenses to be tax-deductible, they must be incurred wholly and exclusively for the purposes

5 *Mason v Innes* (1967) 44 TC 326, CA.
6 TCGA 1992 s 260.
7 TMA 1970 s 16.

of the profession.[8] This condition is much less rigorous than that laid down for employees, whose expenses must be incurred wholly, exclusively and necessarily for the purpose of their employment.[9]

It should be stressed that the expenses detailed below are of a type which may be allowable for a performer who is accepted by the Inland Revenue as self-employed. Where the Inland Revenue is of the view that the performer is undertaking a series of short-term employments (see p 19) then the more stringent expense rules set out in Chapter 3 for employees will apply. The effect of this is that only expenses incurred in the actual performance of the employment will be allowable thereby excluding costs such as subsistence and travel.

Although a strict interpretation of the expense provisions would exclude expenditure which has a duality of purpose in that it provides some personal benefit to the individual, the Inland Revenue, by concession, will often allow an allocation of expenditure which has such a dual nature. Expenses which are partly personal and partly business may therefore qualify for some relief. However, the Inland Revenue's attitude has hardened, particularly in the area of clothing, since the decision in *Mallelieu v Drummond*[10] where it was held that the expenses incurred by a barrister in acquiring clothes for appearing in court, which were also suitable for normal wear, were not deductible.

The following categories of expense will normally be considered deductible by the Inland Revenue when incurred by performers provided they are incidental to the performing activities:

- directly related costs;
- agent's and manager's fees and commissions (see p 58 for deduction for employed performers);
- travel from central base to engagements and competitions; touring and living expenses if supporting a permanent home (see below);
- payment for use of sports facilities;
- taxis to and from the station whilst touring;
- supporting artists;
- singing, dance and sports coaching (including hire of hall – but see below);
- laundry of professional clothing, theatre laundry etc;
- accounting and legal fees;
- professional subscriptions, Equity subscriptions, professional journals;
- cost of professional clothing;
- tips to dressers, call boys, stage doorkeepers etc;
- cost of equipment/instruments etc – normally through a capital allowances claim unless the equipment has a short life;
- cost of repair to wardrobe and props, cleaning of wardrobe and props, cost of replacement or renewal of wardrobe or props;
- insurance re equipment/public indemnity;
- hairdressing;
- cosmetics, make-up;
- chiropody (for dancers, mainly ballet);

8 TA 1988 s 74(a).
9 Ibid s 198.
10 *Mallalieu v Drummond* [1983] STC 665, HL.

- postage and stationery;
- records, books etc;
- medical expenses in connection with 'professional' injuries;
- publicity costs, photographs, blocks etc;
- hire of television set;
- business telephone, telemessages;
- secretarial assistance including possible payments to spouse. Such payments may enable a spouse to utilise his or her own tax reliefs;
- research assistance and material;
- visits to theatre/cinema/concerts/sports events if these are relevant to performer's own profession;
- costs of music, theatre and sporting tickets for agents, managers, press etc;
- overdraft interest.

Relief is available for interest on loans taken out to finance an individual's business or if put into a partnership where the individual is a partner.

In some professions, eg writing or fine art, the individual may incur considerable expense in research and obtaining materials before commencing his first project and it could be argued that this expenditure is preparatory to carrying on the profession, rather than an expense of the profession. It is suggested that, where possible, an advance payment is negotiated to cover such expenses to minimise the risk of there being insufficient income to cover the expense. Relief for such expenditure may also be available under the provisions which allow pre-trading expenditure to be deducted in the first period of trading.[11]

In practice the Inland Revenue will generally allow a proportion of certain costs to be deducted when computing taxable profits. The following are illustrative of this type of expenditure:

- general clothing if required to maintain an 'image';
- use of home as business base: it may be possible to claim a deduction for the use of the performer's home as a business base – this can take the form of either a round sum estimated to cover the running costs, or a more specific calculation can be made if a specific part of the home is used. Careful consideration must be given to the making of any such claim as the use of a home for business purposes may give rise to adverse capital gains tax and rating consequences;
- cosmetic surgery/dentistry;
- subsistence expenditure when on tour.

The following costs will not usually be deductible:

- costs incurred in learning a profession, eg singing lessons prior to taking up professional engagements;
- expenditure on capital assets (see capital allowances on p 41);
- entertaining;[12]
- travel from the performer's home to engagements unless it can be shown that the home is also the 'office';

[11] ICTA 1988 s 401.
[12] TA 1988 s 577.

- an income tax deduction is allowed for VAT incurred on otherwise deductible expenses when the performer is not registered for VAT. If the performer is registered for VAT, he will be able to recover VAT paid by him by completing his VAT return in the usual way.

## Capital allowances

Where a performer incurs expenditure on fixed assets, eg musical instruments, video recorders etc, these qualify for capital allowances.

Expenditure on eligible capital assets, including motor cars, qualifies for a 25% allowance in the year in which it is incurred with the balance being written off on a declining balance basis.[13] This allowance is deducted in calculating taxable profits.

The annual allowance for motor vehicles suitable for private usage cannot exceed £3,000 per annum.[14]

Additionally, expenditure on certain buildings, such as recording studios, may qualify for industrial buildings allowance of 4% per annum or 100% in the year of acquisition for commercial buildings in enterprise zones.[15] The cost of land does not qualify for relief. In practice it is possible to claim a substantial portion of the cost of buildings as plant qualifying for the higher 25% allowance eg air conditioning, lifts, water and heating systems etc.

## Loss utilisation

Currently any trading loss incurred in the exercise of an individual's profession can be relieved in a number of ways:

(1) It can be carried forward against subsequent profits of the profession.[16]
(2) It can be set off against other income in the same year of assessment, and the succeeding year if the profession is still carried on. From 1997/98 under the new rules a loss in an accounting period can be offset against other income in the year of the loss or the preceding tax year.[17]

### *Example*

An individual has been carrying on a profession for several years with the following results:

| | | £ |
|---|---|---|
| Year ended | 30 April 1990 | 18,000 profit |
| | 30 April 1991 | 19,500 loss |
| | 30 April 1992 | 25,000 profit |

13 CAA 1990 s 24.
14 Ibid s 34(3).
15 Ibid s 6(1).
16 TA 1988 s 385(1).
17 Ibid s 380.

His other assessable income consists of:

| | *Dividends* | *Interest* |
|---|---|---|
| | £ | £ |
| 1991/92 | 3,750 | 1,400 |
| 1992/93 | 3,900 | 2,100 |
| 1993/94 | 4,000 | 2,900 |

Strictly the loss should be apportioned over the relevant fiscal years but in practice the loss is normally considered to arise in the year of assessment in which the accounting period ends. Therefore, the loss arises in 1991/92 and can be utilised as follows:

| | | *Without relief* | *With relief* |
|---|---|---|---|
| 1991/92 | Income from profession: | £ | £ |
| | (normal preceding year basis) | 18,000 | 18,000 |
| | Investment income | 5,150 | 5,150 |
| | | 23,150 | 23,150 |
| | Loss relief | - | (19,500) |
| | | 23,150 | 3,650 |
| | Personal allowance | (3,295) | (3,295) |
| | Taxable income | 19,855 | 355 |
| | Tax | £4,963.75 | £88.75 |

The tax saving is £4,875

(3) It can be set off against any capital gains realised by the individuals in the year of assessment.[18]

(4) If a loss is incurred in any of the first four years of assessment following the commencement of the profession, it may be set off against any other income in the three preceding years, earlier years being relieved first. This relief is designed to benefit (although it is not confined to) those persons who were in employment and then start up in business on their own account.[19] The idea is to give tax relief for any initial business losses against their income previously received from employment.

*Example*

An individual commences a profession as a performer on 1 July 1992 and in the period of account to 5 April 1993 has a loss of £5,000. In the year 1992/93 he has salary from employment of £12,000 and in 1991/92, 1990/91 and 1989/90 he earned £10,000, £9,000 and £8,000 respectively. He could use his losses as follows:

[18] FA 1991 s 72.
[19] TA 1988 s 381.

(a) Set off against current year: 1992/93

| | £ |
|---|---|
| Earned income | 12,000 |
| Loss | (5,000) |
| | 7,000 |
| Personal allowance | (3,445) |
| Taxable income | £3,555 |

(b) Set off against earliest previous year: 1991/92

| | £ |
|---|---|
| Earned income | 8,000 |
| Loss | (5,000) |
| | 3,000 |
| Personal allowance | (3,295) |
| Taxable income | Nil |

or

(c) The loss could be carried forward and set off against profits in future years.

## Ceasing to carry on a profession

Once an individual has ceased to carry on his profession, any residual income which arises will continue to be taxed as if it were earned income.[20] Deductions are available for expenses incurred in earning the income.[1] For example, a performer may cease to exercise his profession on the establishment of employment arrangements to improve his tax position. In such circumstances, it is not always practicable to transfer the income rights to the new employer and the amounts will therefore constitute post-cessation receipts in the hands of the performer.

An exception to this general rule is that a lump sum received by an author's executor for the total or partial assignment of copyright in the author's literary, dramatic, musical or artistic work is not liable to income tax.[2]

Although the provisions relating to post-cessation receipts are restrictive, there may be some scope for the renegotiation of contractual entitlements to provide for a more favourable flow of income after an individual's profession has ceased.

## Sales of copyright

There are many occasions when a performer may receive substantial lump sum payments for the disposal of copyrights or similar products. The

20 TA 1988 s 103.
1 Ibid s 105.
2 Ibid s 103(3)(b).

legislation contains both reliefs to enable the spreading of tax over more than one tax year to diminish the incidence of high marginal rates of tax and anti-avoidance measures to prevent the conversion of future income into capital sums.

As explained on p 35 the proceeds of disposal of a performer's copyright will normally be treated as trading income in his hands and subject to taxation on that basis. This can give rise to problems where the pattern of income is irregular. There are, therefore, relieving provisions available which have the effect of spreading the income over a number of tax periods. The only exception to this general rule is where a passive investor purchases a copyright as an investment.[3] The income is then taxed in his hands as unearned income and a gain on sale is treated as a capital gain.

**Extended creation periods**

Where an author assigns or grants an interest by licence in respect of a copyright work, he may claim relief provided the following conditions are met:

(1) The copyright must have been in respect of a literary, dramatic, musical or artistic work of the author.
(2) Consideration for the assignment or grant must consist wholly or partly of a payment which would normally be included in the profits of his profession.
(3) He must have been engaged on the making of the work for more than 12 months.[4]

The relief is as follows:

(1) If he was engaged on the work for a period not exceeding 24 months, only half of the amount will be treated as receivable on the date it was actually receivable and half will be treated as receivable 12 months before that date.[5]
(2) If he was engaged on the work for a period in excess of 24 months, only one third of the amount will be treated as receivable on the date it was actually received, one third is treated as being receivable 12 months previously and one third 24 months previously.[6]

This relief also applies where an author receives a lump sum payment, eg a non-returnable advance of royalties, or a payment on account. It does not, however, apply to payments in respect of the copyright in any work receivable more than two years after its first publication, performance or exhibition.[7]

[3] *Glasson v Rougier* (1944) 26 TC 86, KB.
[4] TA 1988 s 534(1).
[5] Ibid s 534(2).
[6] Ibid s 534(3).
[7] TA 1988 s 534(4).

*Example*

On 30 June 1991 an author receives an advance of £40,000 in respect of a book which he has been writing since April 1989. His other income from writing is:

| *Year ended* | *Income* |
|---|---|
| | £ |
| 30 April 1990 | 16,000 |
| 30 April 1991 | 15,000 |
| 30 April 1992 | 16,000 |

Tax payable without relief:

| | *1991/92* | *1992/93* | *1993/94* |
|---|---|---|---|
| | £ | £ | £ |
| Earnings | 16,000 | 15,000 | 16,000 |
| Advance | - | - | 40,000 |
| | 16,000 | 15,000 | 56,000 |
| Personal allowance | (3,295) | (3,445) | (3,445) |
| Taxable income | 12,705 | 11,555 | 52,555 |
| Tax | £3,176.25 | £2,788.75 | £17,342.00 |
| Total tax | | | £23,307.00 |

Tax payable with relief:

| | *1991/92* | *1992/93* | *1993/94* |
|---|---|---|---|
| | £ | £ | £ |
| Earnings | 16,000 | 15,000 | 16,000 |
| Advance | 13,333 | 13,334 | 13,333 |
| | 29,333 | 28,334 | 29,333 |
| Personal allowance | (3,295) | (3,445) | (3,445) |
| Taxable income | 26,038 | 24,889 | 25,888 |
| Tax | £6,860.20 | £6,300.60 | £6,675.20 |
| Total tax | | | £19,836.00 |
| Saving | | | £3,471.00 |

Any claim to relief under these provisions must be made by 5 April following the expiration of eight years after the work's first publication.[8]

## Sale more than ten years after creation

Where an author assigns or grants an interest by licence in respect of copyright more than ten years after its first publication, he may claim relief provided the following conditions are met:

[8] Ibid s 534(5).

(1) The copyright must be in respect of a literary, dramatic, musical or artistic work of the author.
(2) The consideration for the assignment or grant must consist wholly or partly of a payment which would normally be included in the profits of his profession.
(3) The assignment or grant must be for a period of not less than two years.[9]

The relief is as follows:

(1) Where the copyright or interest is assigned for a period of six years or more, the payment is treated for tax purposes as becoming receivable in six equal annual instalments, the first of which is receivable on the date on which the payment actually became receivable.[10]
(2) Where the copyright or interest is assigned or granted for a period of less than six years, the payment is, for income tax purposes, treated as becoming receivable in equal instalments for each whole year of the period. The first instalment is considered to be receivable on the date on which the actual payment is receivable.[11]

In the event of the death of the author, any outstanding instalment is treated as being receivable on the date of the last instalment before death.[12] If a lower tax charge results, the personal representatives may elect for the tax position to be re-computed for the relevant years on the basis that the assignment or grant was for a period commencing on the actual date on which the payment was receivable and ending on the day before death.[13]

Similarly, if the profession of the author ceases, otherwise than on death, then any outstanding instalment is treated as receivable on the date on which the last instalment before cessation was receivable. The author has the right to elect to have his tax position re-computed as if the assignment or grant was for a period commencing on the actual date on which the payment was receivable and ending with the day before the cessation.[14]

Any claim to relief under these provisions must be made within six years from the end of the tax year in which the payment was receivable.[15] A claim under the relieving provisions in the preceding two paragraphs must be made within two years of death or cessation.[16]

**Artists' receipts**

Similar relief is available for persons whose work is outside the scope of copyright or who work on a fee basis, eg sculptors and artists. If the person

9 TA 1988 s 535(1).
10 Ibid s 535(2).
11 Ibid s 535(3).
12 Ibid s 535(4).
13 Ibid s 535(5).
14 Ibid s 535(6).
15 TMA 1970 s 43.
16 TA 1988 s 535(7).

was engaged in executing the work of art, or a number of works of art, eg for an exhibition, for more than 12 months, he may claim the relief.[17]

The relief is as follows:

(1) If he was engaged in executing the work of art for less than 24 months, half will be treated as receivable on the actual date receivable and half will be treated as receivable 12 months previously.[18]
(2) If he was engaged in executing the work of art for more than 24 months, one third will be treated as receivable on the actual date receivable, one third will be treated as receivable 12 months previously and one third as receivable 24 months previously.[19]

Any claim must be made within six years of the end of the tax year in which the payment was receivable.[20]

## Sale of earnings

Although the above provisions give a measure of relief for certain categories of performer who derive lump sums from the exercise of their profession, there are very few opportunities available to performers to turn their earning capacity into capital sums to avoid income tax. In the 1960s, there were a considerable number of tax mitigation schemes under which a performer could sell his future earnings for a capital sum taxable only at the capital gains tax rate of 30%. These schemes were known as 'constellation schemes' and a number of performers are known to have utilised them. The general principle was that the performer would assign his services to a company in return for shares and then realise a capital gain by disposing of the shares. To prevent such avoidance of tax specific legislation was introduced.[1]

The main provisions of this legislation are as follows:

(1) The legislation sets out to impose income tax on capital sums received by an individual as a result of arrangements under which some other person exploits his earning capacity, and the avoidance or reduction of liability to income tax is the main object, or one of the main objects, of the transaction.[2] This legislation extends to amounts received, as a result of the transactions in question, by persons other than the individual, including cases where the individual has put some other person in a position to receive the capital amount by providing that other person with something of value derived (directly or indirectly) from the individual's activities in the occupation.
(2) Any such capital sum received is treated as earned income of the individual in the tax year it is receivable. It is therefore liable to basic and higher rates of income tax.[3]

17 TA 1988 s 538(1).
18 Ibid s 538(2).
19 Ibid s 538(3).
20 TMA 1970 s 43.
1 TA 1988 s 775.
2 Ibid s 775(1).
3 TA 1988 s 775(2).

(3) The legislation does not apply to a capital amount obtained from the disposal of assets of a profession, a share of a partnership carrying on a profession, or of the shares in a company, providing the amount received is not in excess of the value of the business as a going concern. Any excess over this value is taxed in accordance with this legislation.[4]
(4) The legislation applies not only to UK residents but also to non-residents who carry on an occupation wholly or partly in the UK.[5]

The overall effect of this legislation is to make it extremely difficult to exploit the earning capacity of an individual in return for capital sums. Further, there may less incentive now that the capital gains tax rate is the same as the marginal rate of income tax.

## Capital sums generally

Where capital sums in respect of copyright and similar rights are received by a person not exercising a profession, they will not normally be chargeable to income tax. They will, however, be chargeable to capital gains tax. An example of the type of payment subject to this treatment is the assignment of copyright in consideration for a lump sum by a person who is not a professional author.[6]

Similarly, if a performer receives a capital sum which is ancillary to his professional work, it may not be chargeable to income tax. For example, an actor bought the rights to a film as an investment to compensate him for loss of earnings and subsequently had to sell the rights to a film company before they would make the film. He then starred in the film and received a salary and share of profit from it. The sale of the film rights, however, was held to be capital transaction and not subject to income tax, as it was not part of an actor's profession to dispose of copyrights.[7]

[4] Ibid s 775(4).
[5] Ibid s 775(7).
[6] *Earl Haig Trustees v IRC* (1939) 22 TC 725; *Nethersole v Withers* (1948) 28 TC 501, HL.
[7] *Shiner v Lindblom* (1960) 39 TC 367, Ch D.

# 3 Employed performers

## General arrangements

These can take the form of either independent employment agreements with a 'third-party employer' or of agreements with a 'captive' employer owned by, or connected with, the performer, but which is a separate legal person (eg a company).

Where there is a choice of employment arrangements the performer often forms his own captive employer company which can provide the following advantages:

(1) Significant benefits where extensive time is spent overseas (see p 81).
(2) Where income is earned in an irregular pattern, it can be collected in the company and paid to the individual in a regular pattern, thereby equalising tax rates from year to year, rather than having income in 'peaks' which attract the highest tax rates.
(3) Companies can be used as a simple means of passing wealth to the next generation, in the form of shares in the company.
(4) The protection of limited liability is afforded, although this is restricted as banks, etc may require personal guarantees.
(5) The tax liability on the performer's activity can be deferred if earnings are retained in the company where they will suffer corporation tax at either 25% or 33% as opposed to the higher rates of income tax if the earnings accrue directly to the performer. It will, however, be necessary to deal with the more rigorous reporting and payment requirements for corporation tax under Pay and File which is now in force.

There are, however, also disadvantages to employment arrangements:

(1) PAYE and national insurance must be deducted from any salary paid or made available to the performer in which latter case it may be taxable before it is paid.
(2) The employer must account for NIC on salary paid or made available to the performer.
(3) The employer must comply with the rigorous PAYE and P11D filing procedures.

It is useful to summarise the after tax income available to a performer depending on the legal entity and types of payment involved.

The examples below illustrate the amount which a performer would retain after tax and national insurance for different contractual arrangements at the two extremes of earnings. The first shows the position where a performer earns a marginal £1,000 and his earnings remain below the maximum threshold for employee's Class 1 national insurance. The second shows the position where the marginal £1,000 is for someone whose profits are above the threshold where a company would pay the full rate of corporation tax.

In each case the following alternatives are considered:

(1) The performer is self-employed paying Class 4 NIC.
(2) The performer is employed by a captive company and the earnings are paid out as additional salary.
(3) The performer is employed by a captive company and the earnings are paid out as a dividend.
(4) The performer is employed by a captive company and the earnings are rolled up and eventually distributed as a liquidation distribution.

| | *Self-employed* | *Company via salary* | *Company via dividend* | *Company via capital gain* |
|---|---|---|---|---|
| | *£* | *£* | *£* | *£* |
| *Earnings less than £22,360 pa* | | | | |
| Income to company | — | 1,000 | 1,000 | 1,000 |
| Salary | — | (907) | — | — |
| Employer's NIC | — | (93) | — | — |
| Corporation tax | — | — | (250) | (250) |
| Dividend | — | — | (750) | — |
| Retained by company | — | — | — | 750 |
| Received by individual | 1,000 | 907 | 750 | 750 |
| Class 4/Employee's Class 1 NIC | (73) | (91) | — | — |
| Income tax at 25% | (249) | (227) | — | — |
| Capital gains tax at 25% | — | — | — | (188) |
| Retained by individual | 678 | 589 | 750 | 562 |
| *Earnings more than £1,500,000* | | | | |
| Income to company | — | 1,000 | 1,000 | 1,000 |
| Salary | — | (907) | — | — |
| Employer's NIC | — | (93) | — | — |
| Corporation tax | — | — | (330) | (330) |
| Dividend | — | — | (670) | — |
| Retained by company | — | — | — | 670 |
| Received by individual | 1,000 | 907 | 670 | 670 |
| NIC (none payable as threshold exceeded) | — | — | — | — |
| Income tax | (400) | (363) | (167) | — |
| Capital gains tax at 40% | — | — | — | (268) |
| Retained by individual | 600 | 544 | 503 | 402 |

These are straightforward examples of extreme positions and in deciding the most appropriate arrangements other factors need to be taken into account:

(1) If extensive periods of time are to be spent overseas, employment arrangements provide the opportunity to obtain the 100% deduction (see p 81).
(2) The individual's cash needs have to be taken into account.
(3) If funds are taken in the form of dividends it is difficult to provide for retirement in a tax efficient manner.

Appendix IV summarises the main tax and commercial points to be considered in deciding whether to use a captive employer company. It may be that in the early years the performer should be self-employed, incorporating his activities later when profits have grown. The tax aspects of incorporating have already been discussed on p 30.

Where an individual is employed by a company, the arrangements can take one of two main forms:

(1) The individual's products and services can belong absolutely to the company with the individual being paid emoluments for providing the products or services. The emoluments can be either a pre-determined flat salary or remuneration related to the earnings attributable to his product or services, or a combination of both.
(2) Alternatively, the individual can merely assign his product to the company for a pre-determined period, retaining the absolute interest for himself. He can then be remunerated as in (1) above. This type of arrangement has the advantage that the rights to the product can revert to the individual at the end of the employment period with no tax cost, whereas this can be difficult to achieve under the arrangements in (1) above as the value of the rights could be taxable if returned to the performer in that case.

## Employment conditions

Where an individual has entered into employment arrangements, particularly with a company with which he is connected, he must be careful to ensure that there is a valid and legally binding employment contract and that its terms are adhered to in practice. Otherwise it may be argued by the Inland Revenue that he is continuing to exercise his profession as a self-employed individual or employed by the person with whom his 'captive company' contracts.

## Elements of employment

There is no fixed guideline for determining the conditions necessary to ensure that a contract will be considered a valid employment contract, ie a contract of service. In normal circumstances, however, it would be expected that the following elements would be present to ensure that it is construed as a contract 'of service' (ie master/servant relationship) rather than one 'for services':

(1) The employer must have the power to control the manner in which the functions of the employee are performed. The corollary to this is that the employee must act in accordance with the instructions of the employer.
(2) The contract should be specific as to the services which the employee is required to render. It should refer to the exclusiveness of the services, in that the employee is not allowed to perform them for another party. It is not, however, inappropriate for contracts to be made on a territorial basis, ie UK only, provided the services are exclusive within that territory.
(3) The employer should be entitled to determine the third party to which the employee's services and product are to be made available. The employee may retain a right of approval, but this right should not be such that it negates the employer's control over the employee.
(4) It is preferable that the contract provide for a fixed level of remuneration payable at regular intervals. Additionally, the contract may provide for the payment of bonuses, either linked to the income produced by the employee or at the employer's discretion. The availability of such bonuses may affect the employee's tax status in certain overseas taxing jurisdictions (see p 142).
(5) Although the law does not prescribe a minimum fixed period for employment contracts, it is recommended that they are drawn up for a minimum service period of several years. The terms of the contract can provide for it to continue beyond the termination date, subject to specific notice being given by either party. It is important that the employing company is given sufficient rights under the terms of the employment contract to allow it to enter into valid contracts with other parties, eg record companies etc.

The Inland Revenue has published a general leaflet IR56 which identifies some of the factors which they regard as critical.

Where the employee also controls the company by whom he is employed, care must be taken to maintain the separate identities of company and employee.

Particularly where sportsmen are concerned, there is often the necessity to comply with a controlling body's particular rules relating to employment agreements. These rules as to the form of the contract can reduce flexibility. A good example is professional football where the rules of the English Premier and Football Leagues and English Football Association specify a standard form of agreement for professionals which contains terms relating to expiry of contracts, matches, and out-of-pocket expenses.

They also require all forms of remuneration and benefits to be paid to the player and to be included in the agreement. In addition there are extensive and detailed rules concerning the registration of players and transfer procedures including special provisions which apply on the expiry of a player's contract. These rules effectively mean that professional footballers in the English Leagues are treated as employees for legal and tax purposes. The rules state that all contracts of employment between a club and not only players but also any officials, managers, coaches or trainers must specify that all earnings are to be paid to the individual concerned and not to any company or agency acting on behalf of the employee.

Rules such as these may make it difficult or even impossible to use a captive employer company controlled by the individual. They may also dictate the taxability of a payment, eg a footballer was held to be assessable on the proceeds from his testimonial, principally because the testimonial arose under the then rules of the Football League after a specified number of years of playing service. Furthermore, it is understood that in one case a professional footballer has unsuccessfully argued that for tax purposes he is employed by his own company, although his contract registered with the football authorities is between him and his club. It is understood that the argument was put forward that he acted as an agent of his own company although the Inland Revenue successfully maintained before the Commissioners that there was an employment relationship directly with the club, the earnings from which were subject to PAYE.

The position in other sports is not always as strict as that in football. Thus, for example, county cricketers are allowed under the Test and County Cricket Board's rules to use their own captive employer companies.

## Basic rules

Taxable employment income includes all kinds of payment for work done, eg salaries, fees, commissions, bonuses, perquisites and allowances.[1] Liabilities of the employee met by the employer constitute taxable emoluments together with:

(1) reimbursements of, or allowances for, expenses (subject to a claim to deduct expenses incurred;[2] – see p 58)
(2) contributions by the employer to secure retirement benefits, unless the retirement scheme is approved by the Inland Revenue;
(3) benefits derived by an employee from the use of his employer's assets.

There are certain categories of income which may be outside the charge to income tax, eg:

(1) Non-contractual termination payments of £30,000 or less.[3] To be taxed under these special provisions the payment must not be taxable under any other head. Thus, if the payment constitutes ordinary earnings, the special rules will not apply. This may be the case if, for example, a sportsman was promised the payment at the end of his contract. In this connection the Inland Revenue have been concerned as to what

1 TA 1988 s 131(1).
2 Ibid s 198.
3 TA 1988 s 188.

it considered to be an abuse in football where taxable signing-on fees were being converted to termination payments which were tax free or taxed at a very much lower rate. When a player was transferred from one club to another, ordinarily his new club would have paid him a signing-on fee spread over the period of his new contract. Rather than doing this the new club paid an increased transfer fee to his old club. He then received a termination payment from his old club described as being either in respect of the early termination of his contract or as an ex gratia payment.

The position was reviewed in the case of *Shilton v Wilmshurst*[4] where Peter Shilton was transferred from Nottingham Forest to Southampton. It was accepted that the signing-on fee paid to him by Southampton was taxable but he argued that the payment made to him by Nottingham Forest was tax free. This payment was made to induce him to join Southampton and taxable as an emolument even though Nottingham Forest had no interest in his employment with Southampton and made the payment to secure the transfer fee. The House of Lords held that an emolument 'from employment' meant an emolument 'from being or becoming an employee'.

It is understood that the Inland Revenue continues to look very carefully at all termination payments made to professional footballers with a view to taxing them as ordinary earnings, arguing that the footballer is contractually entitled to these payments. Great care is required in this area.

The making of an ex gratia payment on the occasion of an employee's retirement may also be regarded as a 'relevant benefit' within TA 1988 s 612. If this is the case then the payment will be taxable and not eligible for the £30,000 exemption. Full details of the Inland Revenue's view are set out in SP 13/91 and also ICAEW Technical Release 15/92.

(2) Testimonials and benefits received by performers. These occur primarily in the two major sports of football and cricket although they are now more common in cricket than they are in football. This is probably because the footballers themselves are much better paid than hitherto and cricketers are relatively less well paid. However, there are situations where a footballer has been playing for the same club for a number of years and the club may want him to have a testimonial. The relevant permissions from the football authorities should be sought before doing this but this does not usually create difficulties. On the other hand, in cricket, it sometimes happens that a particular county will have players having benefit years in consecutive years. Further, the better known and long playing cricketers can often have two benefits.

The commercial position has changed somewhat since the original tax cases were decided in the courts. The fund-raising exercises in connection with benefits and testimonials now comprise much more than merely the proceeds of ticket sales from a single cricket or football match plus the money taken from the collection boxes which were the subject of these cases.[5] It is not unusual to find more than a dozen

[4] *Shilton v Wilmshurst* [1991] STC 88, HL.

[5] *Reed v Seymour* (1927) 11 TC 625, HL; *Davis v Harrison* (1927) 11 TC 707, KB; *Moorhouse v Dooland* (1954) 36 TC 1, CA.

fund-raising events during the sportsman's benefit or testimonial year. These can include matches, dinners, dinner-dances, golf days, snooker evenings, discotheques and celebrity football matches. In addition other money will be raised from auctions, raffles, benefit brochures, the sale of ties and other souvenirs. The sportsman and his committee often spend a significant amount of time on these activities.

Perhaps, now more than ever, careful attention should be paid to the tax and other aspects. Thus, for example, adherence to football and cricket rules dealing with testimonials and benefits is important. Proper legal advice should be taken in difficult areas, for example, to what extent it is permissible to use lotteries and raffles to raise money in view of the provisions of the Lotteries and Amusements Act 1976.

In recent years, monies derived by sportsmen from benefits and testimonials have been accepted as being free of income tax. However, it should not be assumed that this will continue to be the case and proper planning should be undertaken. The Inland Revenue could attempt to tax the proceeds under the following heads:

(a) by arguing that the proceeds are ordinary earnings;
(b) if the monies are received in connection with the termination of a sportsman's employment, the excess over £30,000 could be taxed;
(c) if there is a trading activity, taxable under Schedule D, Case 1.

Value added tax will also need to be considered, with registration being effected and VAT charged in appropriate circumstances.

Both the Professional Footballers Association and the Test and County Cricket Board have taken legal advice on this matter and have been able to give guidance on the whole question of the taxation of benefits and testimonials, dealing particularly with the risk of being regarded as trading by the Inland Revenue.

It is considered that the exposure will be minimised if certain guidelines are followed:

(a) The club should have nothing to do with the arrangements other than granting its permission. If of necessity the club does get involved, eg in providing administrative support, then a charge should be made to the committee for these services. Any necessary permissions must, however, be sought and obtained by the club.
(b) A committee should be established independently of the club. Neither the player, directors or manager should be members of this committee.
(c) Any club board minute authorising the benefit should be carefully recorded.
(d) Proper minutes of benefit committee meetings should be kept.
(e) Such meetings should not be held at the club's premises.
(f) The player's contract should not contain any rights to a benefit, neither should there be any enforceable agreement for him to have one. Functions additional to the match itself should be limited as far as possible. Where there are such functions the bulk of the 'profit' should be derived from raffles, auctions etc and not on the price of the tickets.

(g) To the extent possible money should be raised by way of donation.
(h) Any trading of merchandise, souvenirs etc and advertising revenue from brochures should be minimised. If substantial income is expected from this source consideration should be given to organising this activity separately so as not to prejudice the treatment of the net proceeds from the other activities.
(i) The player should be involved as little as possible in organising the various activities and certainly not run the activities himself.
(j) Match programmes should be specially printed and distinguishable from the normal match programmes.
(k) Any posters/written material concerning the benefit event should make it clear that it is being organised by an independent committee.

Finally, the clubs themselves can help protect benefits and testimonials from taxation by not awarding them on a regular basis. If they are awarded only to particularly popular and deserving players who have been with the club a long time then the case for arguing that the net proceeds are not in terms of reward for any trading activity, but to give the public the opportunity of expressing their gratitude to the player in a personal capacity, will be reinforced. It appears that the Inland Revenue is no longer content to accept that the proceeds from benefits and testimonials are not subject to tax. It cannot be guaranteed that a particularly successful sportsman will not be challenged in the future. Committees should therefore pay particular attention to the possible tax exposure in organising fund-raising exercises.

(3) Inducement payments (but not signing-on fees paid to professional footballers) provided these are not in fact payments for future services[6] (see p 54). In certain cases, however, capital gains tax and possibly value added tax may be payable.
(4) Prizes and voluntary payments. Prizes are normally taxable where the performer participates with the prize in mind. On the other hand, in the case of sportsmen, the Inland Revenue appears to adopt a pragmatic approach where occasional prizes are received, particularly in the form of trophies. Provided the value of the prize is not substantial it may not seek to tax them. Prizes and voluntary payments are not always taxed, however, as in one Schedule E case an international footballer was held not to be taxable on payments from the English Football Association and a third party following his performances in the 1966 World Cup.[7]

Emoluments from an employment are taxed in the year they are received.[8] A performer is considered to receive emoluments at the earliest of the following:

(1) the time payment is made of or on account of the emoluments;

[6] *Pritchard v Arundale* (1971) 47 TC 680, Ch D.
[7] *Moore v Griffiths* (1972) 48 TC 338, Ch D.
[8] TA 1988 s 202A.

(2) the time when he becomes entitled to payment of or on account of the emoluments;
(3) in the case of a director, when sums on account of the emoluments are credited in the company's records;
(4) in the case of a director, where emoluments are determined for a period before a period ends when the period ends;
(5) in the case of a director where the amount of earnings for a period is not determined until after the period ends, the time when the amount is determined.[9]

## Pay As You Earn (PAYE)

Every employer in the UK is required to deduct tax under the PAYE system on paying remuneration to his employees.[10] This requirement applies whether or not the employer has been directed to do so by the Inland Revenue. The tax deducted must be paid over monthly, or in certain cases quarterly, to the Inland Revenue.

Tax deductions are governed by the cumulative earnings in the relevant pay period and the code number of the employee in relation to official tax tables. The code number reflects the employee's allowances and reliefs. Since 6 April 1993 employees may have negative allowances with the introduction of K codes such that amounts are added to taxable income.

Employers are required to keep records of each employee's pay and must make annual returns to the Inland Revenue. Inland Revenue officers make periodic audits of pay records and Inland Revenue statistics show that three out of four visits find irregularities. In the event of non-compliance with PAYE regulations, the primary liability in respect of the failure to make tax deductions lies with the employer. It is only in exceptional circumstances that the Inland Revenue will seek to collect tax from the employee and in the absence of a specific agreement to the contrary the employer normally has no right of recovery from the employee.

### PAYE: special points

PAYE does not normally apply to remuneration paid in kind, eg the benefit an employee derives from the use of a house owned by the employer. However, with effect from 25 May 1994 regulations have been introduced which require PAYE to be applied where assets or vouchers are made available and these can be turned into cash either by trading on a designated market or through some other trading arrangements.

Employers must submit annually to the Inland Revenue form P11D for each employee earning more than £8,500 pa,[11] detailing such items, except where an Inland Revenue dispensation has been obtained.[12] A facsimile of form P11D is provided in Appendix VI. Assessments are then made

[9] Ibid s 202B.
[10] Ibid s 203.
[11] TMA 1970 s 15.
[12] TA 1988 s 166.

on employees as necessary. In certain cases, adjustments may be made to the PAYE coding instead.

Round-sum expense allowances must be treated as pay for PAYE purposes.

## Expenses

The rules relating to the deduction of expenses incurred by employees are more stringent than those for self-employed individuals. Expenses must be incurred wholly, exclusively and necessarily in the performance of the employee's duties.[13] The effect of these criteria is that deductible expenses are limited to those which each and every holder of the particular employment would necessarily be obliged to incur in actually performing the duties of his office. Deductible expenses would include subsistence expenses, eg, in the case of sportsmen, travel to competitions and away matches and overseas trips and costs. Where a performer is not provided with a company car then reimbursement for business usage in accordance with the rates set out in the Inland Revenue Fixed Profit Car Scheme (FPCS) will not constitute a benefit. The current FPCS rates are:

| | *Cars up to 1,000 cc* | *Cars 1,001–1,500 cc* | *Cars 1,501–2,000 cc* | *Cars over 2,000 cc* |
|---|---|---|---|---|
| Up to 4,000 miles | 27p | 33p | 41p | 56p |
| Over 4,000 miles | 15p | 19p | 23p | 31p |

Sportsmen may also be able to obtain a tax deduction for individual subscriptions to the body representing professionals in the particular sport.[14]

Following the Inland Revenue's attempt to reclassify certain types of performers as employees rather than self-employed relief was introduced for payments of commission by performers.[15] The relief is available where:

(1) the payment is made by the employee who must be an actor, singer, musician, dancer or theatrical artiste to someone acting as an agent under contract;
(2) the agent carries on business as a licensed employment agency; and
(3) the payment is calculated as a percentage of the employee's earnings.

Relief is restricted to 17.5% of the employee's earnings. Relief is also available for fees paid to a bona fide cooperative society acting as agent. The restrictive nature of the relief means no relief is available for fees paid to agents by employed sportsmen, eg footballers.

[13] Ibid s 198.
[14] ICTA 1988 s 201.
[15] Ibid.

## Benefits

In some circumstances, it may be tax effective for the employee to be provided with benefits by his employer, as the latter will obtain a greater deduction for tax purposes than the taxable benefit accruing to the employee.

*Examples*

| *Benefit* | *Tax deduction* | *Taxable benefit* |
|---|---|---|
| Company car | Capital allowances up to £3,000 pa or lease cost (restricted if original market value of car over £12,000) plus running costs. | Based on 35% of the original list price of the car with discounts for age and business mileage.[16] |
| Petrol for private mileage | Cost to company | Between £580 and £1,200 depending on size of car and business mileage.[17] |
| Other company assets, eg television, video, furniture | Capital allowances at the rate of 25% on declining balance | 20% of market value at time provided to employee less any claim for business usage.[18] |
| Loans | Interest paid by company | 7.5% of actual loan outstanding unless loan does not exceed £5,000[19] |

Other tax effective benefits and expenses are:

(1) The provision of living accommodation where the property cost is less than (or in some cases is worth less than) £75,000 – in this event the performer is taxed on the 'annual value' of the property less any rent paid by him. Where the employer owns the property 'annual value' is the gross rateable value.[20] If the property costs more than £75,000 an additional annual charge arises for tax purposes calculated on the excess of the cost over £75,000 at an 'official' rate of interest (currently 7.5% pa).[1]

(2) The payment of removal expenses, eg where an employed sportsman moves his employment between clubs. Such expenses borne by the employer are non-taxable up to £8,000.[2]

16 TA 1988 s 157.
17 Ibid s 158.
18 Ibid s 156.
19 Ibid ss 160, 161.
20 Ibid s 145.
1 Ibid s 146.
2 Ibid Sch 11A para 24.

Removal expense reimbursements not taxed by the Inland Revenue include:

(a) solicitor's fees;
(b) estate agents' fees;
(c) stamp duty on purchase of new house;
(d) transport of household goods;
(e) cost of temporary accommodation in new location.

The following removal-related expense reimbursements are generally taxed by the Inland Revenue:

(a) additional cost of the new house;
(b) central heating;
(c) initial repairs and alterations;
(d) decorations.

Other items provided to sportsmen are, however, likely to be taxed: for example the Inland Revenue is unlikely to accept that the payment of medical insurance premiums is tax free. Thus an argument that, because of the nature of the footballer's or cricketer's duties, it was vital that private medical insurance was taken out, so that the player could receive immediate treatment for his injury privately, was not accepted by the Inspector.

The Inland Revenue may seek to tax the provision of complimentary tickets provided to performers. The practice of providing such tickets is widespread in some sports and sometimes more tickets are provided than are required for the performer's own personal use. In practice, although they are provided for the performer for his own use, they may be sold and thus he can turn them to cash.

## Players' pools

This is a difficult area where it is impossible to generalise. These arrangements usually occur where a team sport is involved and marketing opportunities are greater where the players act collectively. In this event a pool is usually formed to negotiate contracts with commercial organisations on the team's behalf and also to control and distribute the money earned. Sometimes receipts will be in kind and often the pool will be advised and assisted by a consultant who is independent of the sports club or organising body. The sports organisation may get involved to a greater or lesser extent but at the very least it is likely to want to ensure that its reputation is protected and that players in the team do nothing to conflict with their responsibilities on the field of play. Sports organisations may or may not be responsible for handling the money. It is the case in many situations that little regard is paid to the tax liabilities which may arise although the Inland Revenue, particularly in the form of Special Office, will usually be very interested in this sort of pool arrangement as it will want to ensure that there is no loss of tax. In many cases arrangements have been reached with the Inland Revenue for one person to be responsible for the pool and to deduct basic rate tax from payments to pool members and account for this to the Inland Revenue.

In principle the player's income from the pool can be taxed either as:

(1) employment income in respect of his employment with his employing club or from the organising body if it is a national team; or as
(2) trading or other income taxable under Schedule D.

Certainly the player is likely to be taxed on any cash income received from the pool and also on any consideration provided in kind although the quantum of taxable income may depend on whether it is under (1) or (2). One thing certain is that sportsmen who fail to report such income do so at their peril. Further, any sportsman who is a member of the pool organising committee needs to look carefully at his own personal obligations in relation to the funds he receives and distributes out to pool members. He may well find that there is a tax liability but no funds to meet it if the funds have been distributed already.

## National teams

With regard to sportsmen, there is one particular type of engagement not found elsewhere. Invitations to play for the national team. These are worth looking at carefully since they are not usually determined with tax in mind and the legal formalities are often minimal comprising merely an invitation to join the party, setting out brief details of the financial aspects, but going into the travel, training and other arrangements in some depth. Before researching the position from the individual's point of view it is worth contacting the governing body responsible for the national team since they should have considered the tax and national insurance position. In the case of the English Football Association, an agreement has been reached with the Inland Revenue under which international players employed by UK clubs will receive their fees through their employing clubs who will account for PAYE as appropriate. Similar arrangements exist with the Test and County Cricket Board.

Under such arrangements the individual's engagement may be an extension of his employment with the club which continues to employ him so that he is in effect seconded to the national team for a short period. Alternatively, there may be a separate employment or indeed self-employment relationship with the governing body. It is probable that there will be no intention to create an employment relationship legally although this will not be conclusive. Where tax is currently collected directly from the sportsman in practical terms there is no loss of revenue and the Inland Revenue may have no need to test the matter. The national insurance position will also need to be considered carefully.

## Areas of particular Inland Revenue interest

Within the last four years the Inland Revenue Special Compliance Office in Solihull has taken a particular interest in professional sportsmen, particularly those in football and rugby league. Both professional clubs and the sportsmen themselves have been targeted for under-declared PAYE in the case of the former and under-assessed income tax in the case of the latter. In order to pursue their enquiries the officers involved have sought a wide range of information from third parties about the income of sportsmen; this has included:

(1) details of payments made to sportsmen for publications in which they are involved from publishers.
(2) details of cash and clothing made available to sportsmen under sponsorship and endorsement contracts entered into by sportswear manufacturers.

In addition to income from these sources Special Office has taken a particular interest in:

(1) Salary sacrifices where the employer club has contributed an amount equal to the sacrifice into an approved pension scheme.
(2) Payments made offshore, eg to overseas companies located in low tax jurisdictions.
(3) Cash payments, whether made by the employer club or a third party, for wages, bonuses and expenses.
(4) Payments to the player's agent or service company.
(5) Voluntary payments including ex gratia payments, gifts and testimonials.
(6) Expenses and benefits including:
    (a) company credit cards;
    (b) beneficial loans whether from the employer or a third party;
    (c) NIC saving schemes;
    (d) accommodation and transactions between the employer and employee involving property;
    (e) travelling and subsistence expenses particularly those for foreign tours;
    (f) removal expenses.
(7) Fees payable to the sportsmen on transfer from one club to another.

In all cases the Inland Revenue has sought to discover undeclared Schedule E liabilities although in many cases Special Office has sought to collect any tax due from the employer club under PAYE. In Special Office's experience often the documentation is deficient and is not strong enough to avoid Schedule E liability. It certainly seems that sportsmen (and their employing clubs for that matter) are not always well advised. The Special Office investigators have built up considerable industry expertise including knowledge of sports particular rules and are not dislodged from their views easily – sportsmen be warned!

## Reliefs and allowances

Employed performers can take advantage of the usual reliefs and allowances, eg all personal allowances and interest relief on loans to purchase a principal private residence (limited to £30,000).[3] Interest relief may also be available for the purchase of shares in a close company (ie broadly under the control of five or fewer persons) whether or not the company employs them.[4] The main condition to be satisfied is that the performer must own at the time the interest is paid at least 5% of the company's ordinary share capital or own some part of that share capital and also work for the greater part of his time in the actual management or control of the company. The relief also applies where the money borrowed is re-lent to the company for its business. This relief may be of particular interest to a performer owning shares in his employer company which is close.

[3] TA 1988 s 354.
[4] Ibid s 360.

# 4 Retirement planning

A performer's career can be short lived and it is important that the maximum opportunity is taken to provide for his retirement in the most tax efficient way. This chapter covers separately the position relating to pension provision for self-employed and employed performers.

## Self-employed performers

Although the use of personal pension plans and retirement annuity plans is generally regarded as a means of providing retirement funding for the self-employed, such policies can be used for employed performers provided the employer companies do not operate their own pension schemes.

### Pensions

An individual may deduct from his net taxable earnings payments made by him to a personal pension plan to provide him with a pension in old age.[1]

The use of a pension plan can provide a tax efficient method of sheltering income in years of high marginal tax rates. The amounts paid into such a scheme can be invested in a tax-free fund and eventually paid out in a partly non-taxable form and partly as an annuity when the entertainer's level of income has fallen.

The introduction of variants of the traditional self-employed pension schemes has made these even more attractive. Examples of these schemes are discussed below.

### Personal pension plans

A personal pension plan:

(1) Must preclude any payment during the individual's life other than a payment under (3) below or a pension beginning between the ages of 50 and 75. Where it can be shown that it is customary to retire before the age of 50, the pension can commence at an earlier date.[2]

[1] TA 1988 s 639.
[2] Ibid s 634.

Retirement ages have been agreed by the Inland Revenue in respect of the following professions:

| | *Retirement age* |
|---|---|
| Badminton players | 35 |
| Boxers | 35 |
| Brass instrumentalists | 55 |
| Cricketers | 40 |
| Cyclists | 35 |
| Dancers | 35 |
| Footballers (excluding Football League players) | 35 |
| Golfers (tournament earnings) | 35 |
| Jockeys (flat racing) | 45 |
| Jockeys (national hunt) | 35 |
| Motor racing drivers | 40 |
| Newscasters (ITV) | 50 |
| Rugby league players | 35 |
| Singers | 55 |
| Speedway riders | 40 |
| Squash players | 35 |
| Tennis and table tennis players | 35 |
| Wrestlers | 35 |
| Trapeze artists | 40 |

(2) Must preclude any payment after his death, other than a payment under (3) below or a pension to the surviving spouse or a return of contributions plus interest and bonuses.[3]

(3) Can provide that an individual may commute part of the annuity for a tax-free lump sum of up to 25% of the value of the benefits provided by the scheme.[4]

## Limit of deductibility

There is a general limit on the deductibility of contributions of 17.5% of 'net relevant earnings'.[5] Higher limits of 20% to 40% apply to individuals aged over 35.[6]

To the extent that premiums for a year are insufficient to utilise the full amount of relief available, the unutilised relief can be carried forward for up to six years to allow additional relief in the future.[7]

### *Example*

A performer aged under 35 in all years has net relevant earnings, and pays personal pension premiums, as follows:

[3] TA s 633.
[4] Ibid s 635.
[5] Ibid s 640(1).
[6] Ibid s 640(2).
[7] Ibid s 642.

| | *Net relevant earnings* | *Premiums paid* |
|---|---|---|
| | £ | £ |
| 1990/91 | 20,000 | 3,000 |
| 1991/92 | 25,000 | 4,500 |
| 1992/93 | 27,000 | 5,000 |
| 1993/94 | 30,000 | 5,500 |

These can be utilised as follows:

| | *Limitation* | *Amount paid* | *Relief for year* | *Relief available to carry forward* |
|---|---|---|---|---|
| | £ | £ | £ | £ |
| 1990/91 | 3,500 | 3,000 | 3,000 | 500 |
| 1991/92 | 4,375 | 4,500 | 4,500 | 375 (500–125) |
| 1992/93 | 4,725 | 5,000 | 5,000 | 100 (375–275) |
| 1993/94 | 5,250 | 5,500 | 5,350 | – |

Note that no relief can be obtained for £150 (£5,500–£5,350) of premiums paid in 1993/94 as this exceeds the annual limitation plus relief brought forward. The excess premium would have to be repaid.[8]

**Payment of premiums**

Premiums must be paid in the year of assessment. Premiums paid in the year following the year of assessment may, however, by election, be treated as having been paid in the previous year of assessment.[9] The tax rules do not require premiums to be paid for a set period and therefore single premium policies can be executed each year. This is advantageous for performers with fluctuating levels of income.

Up to 5% of net relevant earnings can be paid to purchase temporary life assurance provided that the overall payments do not exceed the percentage limits described above.[10] This means that life cover can attract relief at the performer's marginal rate of tax up to 40% whereas no relief is available in respect of other life insurance policies taken out after 13 March 1984.

'Net relevant earnings' comprise earnings from an individual's employment or profession less relevant business deductions including capital allowances and overdraft interest[11] and cannot exceed £76,800.[12] The deduction given against earnings for work done overseas (see p 81) does not reduce net relevant earnings. As a result, earnings on which no tax may have been paid can be used in the calculation of net relevant earnings available to carry forward and increase the amount eligible for relief in subsequent years.

It should be noted that if the performer is employed then the contributions to the personal pension plan can be made by the employer, subject to

8 TA 1988 s 638(3)(b).
9 Ibid s 641.
10 Ibid s 640(3).
11 TA 1988 s 646.
12 Ibid s 640A.

the same limitations applying to employee contributions[13]. Such payments do not constitute earnings for national insurance purposes[14] and it can therefore be preferable for payments to be made by the employer rather than the employee.

**Retirement annuity premiums**

Prior to the introduction of personal pension plans, retirement funding for the self-employed was normally carried out through the medium of retirement annuity premiums. These were annuity contracts entered into prior to 1 July 1988 which provided for:

(1) A payment of a pension to the individual paying the premiums beginning between the ages 60 and 75.[15] As is the case for personal pension plans, earlier retirement was allowed for certain professions.[16]
(2) A payout of a pension to a surviving spouse or a return of contributions plus interest and bonuses on death.[17]
(3) The individual could elect to commute part of the annuity for a tax-free lump sum of up to three times the annual amount of the remaining part of the annuity. For contracts entered into between 17 March 1987 and 30 June 1988, the lump sum was capped at £150,000 per policy.[18]

Contracts entered into prior to 1 July 1988 can be continued. Relief is allowed in the same way as for personal pension plans but relief is only given up to 17.5% of net relevant earnings for individuals up to age 50.[19] Individuals over 50 can get relief at between 20% and 27.5% of their net relevant earnings.[20] However, there is no cap on net relevant earnings.

Where relief is available for both retirement annuity and personal pension premiums the relief for personal pension contributions is reduced by the amount of relief given for retirement annuity contributions.[1]

**Self-invested personal pension schemes**

A number of insurance companies now offer pension schemes for the self-employed under which premiums are invested in a private plan which gives the individual or partners the ability to manage the pension fund themselves in conjunction with an investment manager appointed by the company.

13 Ibid s 643.
14 Social Security (Contributions) Regulations 1979 SI 1979/591 reg(1)(k).
15 TA 1988 s 621(3)(b).
16 Ibid s 621(4).
17 Ibid s 621(3)(c).
18 Ibid s 618(2).
19 Ibid s 619(2).
20 Ibid s 626.
1 Ibid s 655(1).

# Employed performers

## Pensions

As in the case of personal pension plan schemes, the use of an Inland Revenue approved pension scheme can be advantageous in providing a method of sheltering income in years of high marginal tax rates. The contributions paid by both the employer and employee can be invested in a tax-free fund to provide a pension on the employee's retirement.

Where Inland Revenue approval has been obtained for a pension scheme, the following advantages arise over a non-approved scheme.

(1) The employee is not taxed on his employer's contributions to the scheme.[2]
(2) Investment income and capital gains of the scheme are not subject to tax.[3]
(3) Up to 150% of final salary can be taken by the employee on retirement as a tax-free lump sum subject to 20 years' service with the company.[4] This option will result in a reduction in the periodic pension payable, the maximum level of which is two-thirds of final salary before any commutation.[5]
(4) The employer obtains corporation tax relief for his contributions.[6]
(5) The employee obtains tax relief at his marginal rate for any personal contribution up to 15% of salary.[7]

For members who joined a scheme on or after 1 July 1989, the maximum salary taken into account when calculating the above limits is £76,800.[8]

A retirement benefit scheme includes any scheme, deed or arrangement (even if for a single employee or even if the pension is to commence immediately) which provides benefits on retirement, but excludes benefits payable on account of disablement or death by accident during service.

## Conditions for approval

The following conditions must be satisfied for a scheme to receive approval. The Inland Revenue, however, has a discretion to dispense with any of the conditions.

(1) The scheme must relate to a trade carried on in the UK by a person resident in the UK.[9] A resident person has to be responsible for administering the scheme.[10]

2 TA 1988 s 596(1).
3 Ibid s 592(2), (3); TCGA 1992 s 271(1)(g).
4 TA 1988 s 590(3)(d).
5 Ibid s 590(3)(a).
6 Ibid s 592(4).
7 Ibid s 592(7)(8).
8 Ibid s 590C.
9 TA 1988 s 590(2)(e).
10 Ibid s 590(2)(c).

(2) The employer must contribute to the scheme[11].
(3) The employer and relevant employees must recognise it.[12]
(4) The employee's contributions must not be returnable in any circumstances before normal retirement date.[13]
(5) The sole purpose of the scheme must be to provide employees, or their widows, children, dependants or personal representatives with pensions, lump sums, gratuities or similar benefits.[14]

## Summary of benefits

An Inland Revenue approved scheme will normally permit the following benefits:

(1) A pension on retirement between the ages of 60 and 70 which must not exceed two-thirds of the employee's 'final remuneration' if 20 years' service has been completed.[15] It is understood that, in the case of certain performers, agreement has been reached with the Pensions Schemes Office (PSO) under which a pension scheme can be set up to provide a pension at a much lower retirement age. To obtain PSO agreement to any such variation, it is necessary to demonstrate that it is either inadvisable on medical grounds or impracticable for the performer to continue in his profession beyond a certain age. Where substantially earlier than normal retirement ages are agreed, the PSO may require that entitlement to benefits is restricted, eg the short service provisions may not be available.
(2) A widow's pension not exceeding two-thirds of any pension payable to the employee.[16]
(3) Death in service benefit not exceeding four times final remuneration.[17]

No pension can be surrendered, commuted or assigned except in so far as the scheme allows an employee on retirement to obtain a lump sum. This can be the higher of $\frac{3}{80}$ of final remuneration for each year of service or $2\frac{1}{4}$ times the initial pension payable before any commutation and cannot, in any event, exceed 150% of final salary.[18]

## Membership

Membership of an approved scheme has to be confined to employees of the participating employer. The term 'employee' includes, in the case of companies, any officer, director or manager of the company. It is not necessary that membership should be open to all employees in the employer's service or to any particular category of employee. A scheme may, in fact,

11 Ibid s 590(2)(d).
12 Ibid s 590(2)(b).
13 Ibid s 590(2)(f).
14 Ibid s 590(2)(a).
15 IR12 para 7.4.
16 TA 1988 s 590(3)(b).
17 Ibid s 591(2)(c).
18 IR12 paras 8.5, 8.6.

relate to a single employee or to individuals selected on a discretionary basis.

Where an employee is temporarily absent from employment, he may remain in full membership of an approved scheme even though no remuneration is paid during his absence, provided that the employer/employee relationship is regarded as continuing.[19] No limit is normally set on the period of absence if it is caused by ill health, provided that there is an expectation that the employee will return to service.[20] Absence for other reasons should not normally exceed three years.[1]

## Employee contributions

Contributions may not exceed 15% of the employee's taxable remuneration.[2] Such contributions reduce taxable earned income. In some circumstances, it can be beneficial for the employer to make additional emoluments available to the employee enabling him to pay greater contributions personally. Although the overall effect on both the company's and the individual's tax situation is neutral, larger pension benefits will be available to the individual.

### *Example*

An individual is employed by a company at a salary of £25,000 pa. The company has fully funded his pension entitlement to date by means of a non-contributory pension scheme.

If the company were to increase his salary to £29,412 pa and allow him to contribute to the scheme, the tax position for the employee would be the same, but his maximum pension benefits would be increased:

| *Tax position* | *Before increase* £ | *After increase* £ |
|---|---|---|
| Salary | 25,000 | 29,412 |
| Voluntary contribution (limited to 15%) | – | (4,412) |
| Taxable | 25,000 | 25,000 |
| Pension benefits | | |
| Pension (⅔ × salary) | 16,667 | 19,608 |
| Widow's pension (4/9 × salary) | 11,111 | 13,072 |
| Lump sum commutation (1½ × salary) | 37,500 | 44,118 |
| Death-in-service (4 × salary) | 100,000 | 117,648 |

Where the scheme rules permit additional voluntary contributions (AVCs) can be made by the employee, thus providing both with a very flexible tax efficient investment vehicle.

19 IR12 para 3.11.
20 Ibid para 3.13.
1 Ibid para 15.8.
2 TA 1988 s 592(8).

## Employer contributions

Although the employer must contribute to the scheme, there is no minimum contribution requirement. Ordinary annual contributions are immediately tax deductible. Any special contribution to secure back service benefits for past services or to make up an actuarial deficiency in the scheme will have to be spread if it exceeds £25,000. The period of the spread is determined by the size of the special contribution and is as follows:[3]

| | |
|---|---|
| £25,000 - £50,000 | 2 years |
| £50,001 - £100,000 | 3 years |
| £100,000 + | 4 years |

Additionally, it may be tax efficient for the employee to sacrifice remuneration, eg a bonus, with the employer making a contribution to the employer's pension fund. Great care is needed here to ensure that the sacrifice is tax effective.

The Inland Revenue have challenged the effectiveness of salary sacrifice arrangements in one particular sport and have acknowledged the difficulty of the legal issues involved. Guidance had been issued by the Pension Schemes Office in its Memorandum No 54 dated August 1978 (as amended) and Special Office have indicated that in accordance with that guidance for a salary sacrifice to be successful it has:

(1) to be evidenced in writing and signed and dated by the employee contemporaneously;
(2) to constitute a valid variation of the employee's right to remuneration which both the employee and employer regard as binding; and
(3) not to be retrospective.

In that particular case a format for the sacrifice letter which the Inland Revenue would regard as effective was agreed. Two other points of interest arose from the negotiations with the Inland Revenue.

(1) Initially Special Office argued that fees payable for signing the employment contract ('signing on' fees), but payable in instalments over the life of the contract, were not capable of being sacrificed.
(2) Special Office argued that the salary sacrifice could not be made in consideration of a payment into the pension scheme.

Tax counsel's opinion was that Special Office was wrong on both points; Special Office subsequently conceded that future instalments of signing on fees could be sacrificed but did not concede the second point. In practice it would be wise to accept the Inland Revenue view. Substantial sums of tax may be at stake and it is therefore worth taking some care in order to avoid subsequent problems.

3 IR12 para 5.7.

### Funding

There is no requirement for employees to contribute to a scheme in order for it to be approved. For a scheme to be approved, it is necessary to satisfy the Inland Revenue not only that the rules of the scheme limit the benefits payable, but that the funding (ie the rate at which money is being accumulated for the purposes of the scheme) is not excessive. No objection is raised to a reasonable reserve in the funds of approved schemes, but approval may be withdrawn if large surpluses are held unless acceptable proposals are forthcoming to deal with them, eg by reducing contributions or by increasing benefits within approvable limits. Where pension scheme surpluses are repaid to the employer these will be subject to tax at 40% with no offsetting reliefs being available.

### Maximum pension benefits

The aggregate benefits payable to an employee who retires at normal retirement age after 40 years' service with the same employer must not exceed two-thirds of his final remuneration. The basic maximum accrual rate is $^{1}/_{60}$th of final remuneration for each year of service, up to a maximum of 40.[4] An accelerated accrual rate is available to an employee aged 50 or over who has completed 20 years' service.

'Final remuneration' may be computed on either of the following bases:

(1) remuneration for any one of the five years preceding normal retirement date; or
(2) the average of the total earnings for any three or more consecutive years ending not earlier than ten years before the normal retirement date.[5]

Basis (1) cannot be applied to a director who has control of more than 20% of the voting rights of the company.[6]

'Remuneration' for this purpose means basic pay, eg, salary for the year in question, plus the average over a suitable period (usually three or more years) of any fluctuating earnings. Benefits in kind may be taken into account where they are assessed to tax.[7]

### Lump sum benefits and commutation

A scheme will not be approved if the lump sum element in the total benefits at normal retirement age exceeds the higher of (a) $^{3}/_{80}$ths of final remuneration for each year of service up to a maximum of $^{120}/_{80}$ths (150% at the end of 40 years) or (b) $2\frac{1}{4}$ times the initial pension payable before any commutation.[8]

4 TA 1988 s 590(3)(a).
5 IR 12 Appendix 1.
6 Ibid.
7 Ibid.
8 IR 12 paras 8.5, 8.6.

Full commutation of a pension may be permitted if, at the time it becomes payable, the recipient is in 'exceptional circumstances of serious ill health'. This phrase is interpreted narrowly. It is not intended to refer to the kind of ill health which merely prevents somebody from working, but to cases where the expectation of life is really very short by comparison with the average for the same age and sex,[9] ie the employee has less than one year to live.

## Benefits on death-in-service

On death-in-service before normal retirement age, a lump sum not exceeding four times the deceased employee's final remuneration may be provided.[10] The lump sum may be paid to the employee's personal representatives or a nominated beneficiary, or distributed at the discretion of the employer or administrator. In addition, a pension may be provided for a widow or, where there is no widow, for a dependant, of an amount not exceeding two-thirds of the maximum pension that could have been approved for the employee if he had retired on grounds of incapacity on the date of his death.[11]

No lump sum benefits may be paid if death occurs after retirement, except for:

(1) any payment due under a guarantee attaching to the pension; or
(2) any sum falling under a life policy or scheme rules that give continued cover on death after retirement. (It must be noted that the value of such cover must be taken into account as part of the employee's retirement benefits available in non-pension form.[12])

## Widows' and dependants' pensions

A widow's pension may be provided in her own right equal to two-thirds of the maximum pension that could be approved for the employee. Alternatively, a similar pension may be provided for a dependant.[13]

## Inflation adjustments

Retirement benefit schemes may be arranged to take account of inflation by advance provisions to cover cost-of-living increases. The allowance made for future estimated rates of increase must be reasonable and the rules must provide for the disposal of any surplus which arises because the estimated increase does not occur.[14]

9 Ibid para 8.16.
10 TA 1988 s 591(2)(c).
11 IR 12 para 11.7.
12 Ibid para 12.1.
13 TA 1988 s 590(3)(b).
14 IR 12 para 13.9.

### Inheritance tax

Lump sum death-in-service benefits can be paid free of inheritance tax. The lump sum is normally distributed at the discretion of the employer or administrator within a class of beneficiaries. The employee can lodge with the scheme administrator a request for the payment to go to a nominated beneficiary.

### Self-administered pension schemes

These are small pension schemes, primarily for one person or a few people within a company, and thus may be ideally suited to an employed performer.

These schemes, sometimes known as 'captive' pension schemes, can be highly tax efficient. At the same time, they can provide the employee with the ability to manage the funds invested in accordance with his own wishes. Under current Inland Revenue rules, the pension fund can lend back up to half of its funds to the prospective pensioner's company. It can also purchase a business property to be used by the performer's company for business purposes funded by the contributions made and third party borrowings.

## Funded unapproved retirement benefit schemes (FURBS)

Where the level of contribution which can be made to the Inland Revenue approved schemes mentioned above is restricted because of the earnings cap it may be beneficial to establish a FURBS. These are schemes designed to provide retirement benefits for an individual which do not have exempt approval from the Inland Revenue.

Unlike an approved scheme there is no limit on the level of contribution which the employer can make and these will be tax deductible for the employer. However, the contribution paid to the FURBS is treated as a benefit in kind to the performer but the contribution does not attract employer's or employee's NIC. Once the contribution has been made to FURBS the investment income and capital gains arising from the resultant investments are only subject to income tax at the basic rate. Furthermore, the fund is outside the performer's estate for inheritance tax purposes.

On retirement the entire accrued fund can be paid out to the performer with no further tax liability occurring. The Finance Act 1994 introduced special rules for taxing benefits received from a FURBS which had itself not been wholly taxed in the UK.[15]

Unlike Inland Revenue approved schemes there are no restrictions on the investment policy of a FURBS and they can be a very tax efficient investment vehicle.

[15] FA 1994 s 108.

## Planning

The provision of funds for retirement provides a major opportunity temporarily to convert taxable income into tax-free funds as full tax relief will normally be available for the amount transferred into any pension scheme, and the income and capital gains arising on those funds will accumulate tax free. Tax will, however, be paid on that part of the funds paid out as a pension on retirement. It is often difficult to persuade young performers who are earning substantial amounts of money that they should transfer part of this to a pension fund where it will not be available for their direct use for many years.

One also needs to take into account the different methods of funding which the 'self-employed' and 'employed' pension funds require. The company pension can only pay out final benefits which are a function of final salary (see p 73), and where a performer has peak earnings very early in his career the subsequent lower earnings may well form the basis of calculating his pensionable benefits. In these circumstances, either the level of funding must be reduced or any resultant surplus repaid to the employing company where it will be taxable at a standard 40% irrespective of other reliefs available.[16] The use of a small self-administered company pension scheme with greater investment flexibility may persuade the performer to part with direct control of his earnings in a tax efficient way.

Where, however, a personal pension or retirement annuity scheme is used there is no maximum benefit which can be paid out. The level of funding is determined by the percentage restriction on relevant earnings (see p 66), and where significant amounts are paid into the scheme early in the performer's career these can accumulate tax free to produce a substantial benefit.

Where a performer is employed by more than one company, it is possible to use a differing arrangement for each employer which may create additional flexibility. Where there is a desire to crystallise some of the pension benefits, it may be possible for the performer to take early retirement from one of the employments providing him with access to the pension funds albeit at a lower level of benefits.

[16] TA 1988 s 601.

# 5 Overseas aspects

UK income tax applies to:

(1) all income of UK residents;
(2) the UK source income of non-residents.

Thus, a performer who arranges matters in such a way that he is neither UK resident nor has any income from UK sources will not be liable to pay any UK income tax.

These rules are modified by double tax treaties concluded between the UK and other countries and also by Inland Revenue concession. Special reliefs apply to individuals with overseas domicile.

For tax purposes, the UK comprises England, Wales, Scotland and Northern Ireland, but does not include the Channel Islands or the Isle of Man. It also includes the territorial seas.[1]

## Residence

An individual who normally resides in the UK is treated as remaining resident (and ordinarily resident) here if he goes abroad only for short periods.[2]

Where an individual takes up permanent residence abroad he is treated as remaining resident and ordinarily resident if he returns for substantial periods (ie an average of three months or more a year over a four-year period).[3]

If an individual goes abroad permanently he is regarded as remaining ordinarily resident if he comes to the UK in most years.

### Visitors

Individuals who normally live abroad, and come to the UK only as visitors, are resident if:

(1) they spend 183 days or more in the UK in the tax year (days of arrival and departure are normally ignored for this purpose);[4] or

[1] TA 1988 s 830(1).
[2] Ibid s 334, IR20 para 2.1.
[3] IR20 para 2.7.
[4] Ibid para 3.3.

(2) their visits to the UK have averaged three months or more a year for four consecutive years. An individual who comes to the UK with the intention of making such visits in the future may be treated as both resident and ordinarily resident.[5]

### Ceasing to be resident

If an individual can produce evidence that he has ceased to be resident and ordinarily resident, he is usually so treated on a provisional basis following his departure. Such evidence could, for example, relate to the sale of his UK house and the purchase of an overseas house. Normally, the provisional ruling should be confirmed after he has stayed abroad for a period exceeding a complete tax year and provided that his visits to the UK have not amounted to an annual average of three months or more.

If he cannot produce such evidence, the Inland Revenue will tax him during the three years following departure as provisionally resident. His liability will be adjusted, if necessary, when the final determination is made at the end of three years.[6]

## Ordinary residence

A person who is resident in the UK year after year is ordinarily resident there, ie habitually resident.[7]

An individual may be resident, but not ordinarily resident, for a particular tax year, eg where he normally lives overseas but visits the UK for six months or more in a tax year. On the other hand, an individual may be ordinarily resident, but not resident, for a tax year. The question of whether an individual is ordinarily resident is of particular importance when dealing with income from employment (see p 81).

## Full-time employment abroad

A performer will normally be regarded as not resident and not ordinarily resident in the UK for the period abroad if he leaves for full-time service under a contract of employment and:

(1) all duties of his employment are performed abroad or any duties he performs in the UK are incidental to his duties abroad;
(2) his absence from the UK and the employment itself both extend over a period which includes a complete tax year; and
(3) interim visits to the UK do not amount to six months or more in any tax year or three months or more on average.[8]

5 Ibid.
6 IR20 paras 2.5–2.8.
7 Ibid para 1.3.
8 Ibid paras 2.2, 2.3.

A problem may arise if the performer has to return to the UK to perform duties, eg in the case of a sportsman to play in a match against UK opponents, in which event he may remain resident in the UK unless he can satisfy the Inland Revenue that he meets the normal criteria for non-residence.

## Dual residence

A person may be resident (or ordinarily resident) in two or more countries at the same time by virtue of two different countries' criteria for determining residence. He cannot, however, claim to be not resident (or not ordinarily resident) in the UK merely because in that tax year he is resident in another country.[9]

Where, however, a person is regarded as resident both in the UK and in a country with which the UK has a double tax treaty, there may be special provisions for treating him as a resident of only one of the countries for the purposes of the treaty. This normally has the effect of enabling him to escape tax altogether on most sources in one country and thus avoid the possibility of paying tax in both countries with the need to claim a credit for one country's tax against the other's.

## Visits for temporary employment

Individuals who come to the UK to work for a two-year period are treated as resident from the day of arrival to the day of departure. They are not usually treated as ordinarily resident until they have been in the UK for at least three years. If it is clear from the outset that they intend to be in the UK for three or more years, they will be regarded as resident and ordinarily resident from arrival. Other individuals coming to the UK for employment will not be treated as resident unless they spend six months or more in the UK in a tax year.[10]

Where foreign nationals purchase UK accommodation for their use, they will usually be regarded by the Inland Revenue as ordinarily resident. However, if the accommodation is disposed of within three years of arrival and the individual leaves the UK within that period, he will be treated as not ordinarily resident, if that is to his advantage.[11]

## Domicile

An individual is domiciled in the country in which he has his permanent roots. Domicile is distinct from nationality or residence and, under general law, it is only possible to be domiciled in one place at a time.[12]

[9] IR20 para 1.4.
[10] Ibid paras 3.6–3.10.
[11] Ibid para 3.11.
[12] Ibid para 5.2.

Each individual acquires a domicile of origin at birth, normally that of his father at that time. This domicile is retained until his actions and intentions show that he has acquired a domicile of choice elsewhere.[13]

In order to acquire a domicile of choice, an individual must sever ties with his country of origin and enter another country with the definite intention of making a permanent home there.[13]

A wife's domicile is determined independently of her husband's.[14]

## Relief for time spent overseas

Relief is not available in respect of earnings derived from time spent overseas by self-employed individuals during a year of assessment.

As explained on p 23, self-employed performers are taxed on a preceding year basis of assessment. This provides opportunities for planning where large sums of taxable income have been received in a particular period. If the performer can arrange his affairs in such a way that he is not resident for UK tax purposes in the year of assessment for which that period forms the basis, he may be able to avoid paying UK tax on that income.

Any such arrangements must take into account both the tax implications of establishing residence in a foreign jurisdiction and the commercial and personal constraints which may hinder their success.

Support was given to this strategy in the case of *Reed v Clark*.[15] This case involved Dave Clark who had been the leader of the Dave Clark Five. He spent the whole of 1978/79 out of the UK in order to avoid UK tax on his earnings for the year to 31 December 1977. The Inland Revenue argued that the period of absence of shortly over 12 months was not sufficient to cease UK residence but the case was decided in the tax payer's favour. The case suggests that to establish non-residence in such circumstances it is important for the tax payer to establish a firm base elsewhere. If the tax payer moved from place to place without a permanent home it is likely that the case law relating to mariners,[16] on which the Inland Revenue sought to rely in the *Clark* case, would mean that the individual would be regarding as remaining UK resident.

If such a step is taken, care is necessary to ensure that the profession continues for long enough to take it clear of the cessation provisions[17] (see p 26 and that no part of the profession is carried on in the UK in the period of non-residence).[18]

In order to ensure that significant time spent abroad does not result in unexpected tax consequences, Appendix VIII provides a broad outline of the tax rates in the US, Australia, France, Germany, The Netherlands, Japan and the Republic of Ireland. The Appendix also explains how the various overseas jurisdictions tax income arising to a visiting performer from royalties, tours, books, television appearances etc. The extent of

13 Ibid para 5.5.
14 Ibid para 5.6.
15 *Reed v Clark* [1985] STC 323, Ch D.
16 *Rogers v Inland Revenue* (1879) 1 TC 225, Ex(S).
17 TA 1988 s 63 (prior to amendment by FA 1994).
18 Ibid s 18.

taxation is usually dependent on the terms of the 'royalty' and 'artiste and athlete' clauses of double tax treaties concluded by those countries and this is fully considered. Additionally, Appendix IX contains details of rates of withholding tax for those countries having double tax treaties with the UK.

## Time spent overseas by employees

Where performers who are employees spend extended periods outside the UK, even though they may not become non-resident, a deduction of 100% from earnings is given if the following tests are met.[19]

(1) the employee is resident and ordinarily resident in the UK;[20] and
(2) the duties are performed during a qualifying period of at least 365 days,[1] with restricted return visits of not more than 62 consecutive days[2] or one-sixth of the total period of qualifying absence[3] (see example below).

### Employment duties

The 100% deduction is not given if the duties performed overseas are merely incidental to the duties of the employment carried out in the UK.[4] To determine whether overseas duties are incidental, it is necessary to examine their nature and quality. For example, if the overseas duties merely related to finishing off a record substantially completed in the UK, they would usually be regarded as incidental to the UK job. The 100% deduction would not then be available.

### Qualifying period of absence

A qualifying period of absence must comprise 365 or more consecutive days, whether or not this spans a tax year.[5]

Time spent on holidays will not break a qualifying period of absence from the UK.

### Return visits

Return visits to the UK are ignored where they are not more than:

(1) 62 consecutive days,[6] and

19 TA 1988 s 193.
20 Ibid 1988 s 19(1).
1 Ibid s 193(1)(b).
2 Ibid Sch 12 para 3(2)(a).
3 Ibid Sch 12 para 3(2)(b).
4 Ibid Sch 12 para 6.
5 Ibid s 193(1)(b).
6 Ibid Sch 12 para 3(2)(a).

(2) one-sixth of the total period of qualifying absence.[7]

A qualifying period comprises three elements as shown in the following example:

*Example*

X = a visit abroad consisting entirely of days of absence from the UK
Y = a return visit to the UK of not more than one-sixth X + Y + Z
Z = the next visit abroad

These rules are applied on a continuous basis.

| | |
|---|---|
| X | 40 days |
| Y | 20 days |
| Z | 60 days |
| | 120 days |

Return visit Y is not more than one-sixth of the total relevant days and that cycle therefore constitutes a qualifying period, ie the return visit is ignored. However, if the return visit Y had been 21 days or overseas visit Z 59 days, the one-sixth test would not have been met.

Employed performers should ensure as far as practicable that their UK return visits are minimised, particularly in the early stages of overseas engagements as this will ensure that there is some leeway if unexpected visits have to be made to the UK during the course of the year.

## Qualifying days

An employee is absent if he is outside the UK at midnight on the relevant day.[8]

## Qualifying earnings

Where the duties of an employment (including an associated employment) are performed:

(1) wholly outside the UK, the entire earnings qualify for relief;
(2) partly in and partly outside the UK, the earnings qualifying for the 100% deduction are such an amount as is shown to be reasonable having regard to the nature of the duties and the time devoted to them in the UK and abroad and to all other relevant circumstances.[9] In practice, this means that the Inland Revenue will 'average' earnings from all associated employments and only give the 100% deduction against the fraction represented by the time spent abroad.

7 Ibid Sch 12 para 3(2)(b).
8 TA 1988 Sch 12 para 4; *Hoye v Forsdyke* [1981] STC 711, Ch D.
9 TA 1988 Sch 12 para 2(2).

An employment is associated with another if both are with the same person or with persons associated with each other.[10] Earnings for this purpose comprise all forms of taxable pay, less expenses of the employment.

The calculation of the earnings qualifying for the relief may vary depending on the terms of the employment contract and the way in which remuneration is actually paid to the performer. If the contract of employment is silent on the allocation of remuneration then it will normally accrue on a daily basis and the amount qualifying for relief will be calculated on a time apportionment basis.

### *Example*

X undertakes a qualifying period from 5 October 1992 to 4 October 1993 and has earnings as follows:

| | £ |
|---|---|
| Year to 5 April 1993 | 100,000 |
| Year to 5 April 1994 | 150,000 |

The earnings eligible for the relief would be:

| | |
|---|---|
| 6/12 × £100,000 | 50,000 |
| 6/12 × £150,000 | 75,000 |
| | £125,000 |

Supposing, instead, he was paid a base salary of £75,000 per year and a special bonus for the overseas work of £100,000. The earnings qualifying for relief would be:

| | £ |
|---|---|
| 6/12 × £75,000 | 37,500 |
| 6/12 × £75,000 | 37,500 |
| Bonus | 100,000 |
| | £175,000 |

The position can be further complicated where an individual has continuing earnings derived from activities which took place when he was working overseas during a qualifying period.

### *Example*

Y is a musician employed by two companies UKco Ltd for work in the UK and Offco Ltd for work outside the UK. During the year to 31 March 1993 Y undertakes a qualifying absence and records an album for Offco Ltd outside the UK for which Offco Ltd receives a substantial advance of royalties. The major part of this is paid out to Y as remuneration for the year to 31 March 1993 and qualifies for the foreign earnings deduction. In the year to 31 March 1994 Y works outside the UK performing at concerts for which Offco Ltd derives income. Additionally

10 Ibid Sch 12 para 2(3).

the sale of the album recorded in the previous year generates significant income for Offco. Again Offco pays out the bulk of its profit to Y.

It is arguable that part of the remuneration received by Y, ie that derived from the record royalties earned by Offco, is attributable to the qualifying absence and therefore qualifies for the 100% deduction. To maximise the potential of successfully obtaining such a deduction part of the payment of the remuneration to Y should be classified as a bonus relating to the previous year.

Provided the arrangements are structured properly the Inland Revenue will accept that such earnings are eligible for the 100% deduction although negotiations may have to take place over the quantum. The Inland Revenue will argue that a proportion of the earnings of Offco from record sales in subsequent years are attributable to Y's touring and other promotional activities and this can dilute the element qualifying for the relief.

It should be noted that this relief is only available to employees and no corresponding relief is available to self-employed individuals. For this reason, if a performer expects to spend considerable periods of time overseas, but not enough to become non-resident, it may be worthwhile his being employed rather than continuing as self-employed.

Where an entertainer spends more than 60 continuous days in employment outside the UK, he will be permitted a tax deduction for the travelling expenses of up to two trips in a year for his spouse and infant children to visit him.

## Non-domiciled individuals

Individuals who are resident in the UK but not domiciled here are taxable on income derived from the UK but income derived from overseas is only taxable if remitted to the UK.

If the individual is self-employed as a sole trader then all income of his profession is taxable in the UK whether the services are performed in or out of the UK. This is because the Inland Revenue do not accept that it is possible to carry out separate professions in this way.

Similarly, if an individual has a single contract of employment covering duties in and out of the UK then he will be taxable in the UK on all earnings derived from that employment. However, where a non-domiciled individual has a separate contract of employment with a non-resident employer for his non-UK duties which is independent of his UK contract and he does not actually or constructively remit the earnings from the former to the UK, he will be exempt from UK tax on those earnings.[11]

## Foreign tax suffered

Frequently, when a performer performs overseas or receives income from overseas, he will be subject to tax in the foreign jurisdiction (see Appendix

[11] TA 1988 s 19(1).

VIII and p 80). Relief may be available for the foreign tax suffered under the terms of the relevant tax treaty or under the UK unilateral relief provisions.

This latter relief is restricted to the lower of the foreign tax suffered and the UK tax suffered on the foreign income. Each source of income is considered separately and the foreign tax is compared with the marginal rate of UK taxation.[12]

## *Example*

X is an author who receives copyright royalties from Ruritania. In his accounts, made up to 30 April 1992 he includes royalties from this source of £3,000 which have suffered Ruritanian withholding tax of £750. His total earnings in the period amount to £33,000. He pays personal pension premiums of £3,000 in the year ended 5 April 1994.

1993/94 tax payable

| | | | |
|---|---|---|---|
| | | £ | |
| Income | | 33,000 | |
| Personal pension premiums | | (3,000) | |
| | | 30,000 | |
| Personal allowance | | 3,445 | |
| | | £26,555 | |
| | £ | £ | |
| Tax | 2,500 @ 20% | 500 | |
| | 21,200 @ 25% | 5,300 | |
| | 2,855 @ 40% | 1,142 | |
| | £26,555 | £6,942 | |
| Foreign tax credit is the lower of: | | | |
| | £ | £ | |
| | 2,855 @ 40% | 1,142.00 | |
| | 145 @ 25% | 36.25 | |
| | £3,000 | £1,178.25 | |
| | | or £750.00 | |
| | | | (750.00) |
| Tax due | | | £6,192.00 |

In many instances, foreign tax suffered will be set off against the performer's UK income tax liability and, therefore, detailed planning to reduce foreign taxes is not necessary. In certain circumstances, however, eg where the performer is enjoying the benefit of a 365-day qualifying period, or where tax planning has significantly reduced the UK liability, close attention must be paid to the incidence of foreign taxes. It may be possible to reduce foreign taxes by separating out the performance element of any fee from that relating to production costs. This will usually require, at

12 Ibid s 796.

least separate contracts, and, in some cases, a separate company to undertake the production itself.

Additionally, care must be taken to ensure that the foreign tax is suffered, if possible, by a legal entity which can obtain a credit for it in the UK. If, for instance, tax was withheld from a royalty received by a UK company which paid all of its income out to a performer as salary, the foreign tax would be suffered by the company, which would have no UK tax liability against which it could be relieved. In contrast, the performer would have a personal tax liability and would not be able to reduce this by utilising the tax suffered abroad. Similarly, where a performer is appearing overseas the local country will usually have taxing rights under the terms of the treaty. Collection of the tax is often achieved by a withholding deducted by the local promoter and the withholding tax certificate will be issued in the name of the payee. If this is the employer company who is paying the net proceeds out to the performer the tax withheld will not be available to credit against the performer's personal tax liability. It may be possible to get the local tax authorities to agree that the taxable entity is the performer himself as the proceeds ultimately accrue to him. In these circumstances the withholding tax certificates can be issued in his name.

## Overseas profession

If it can be demonstrated that an individual's profession is carried on wholly abroad, profits are taxed under Schedule D, Case V on the remittance basis.[13] It is extremely difficult for a performer resident in the UK to show that his profession is carried on wholly abroad and it is not possible, for tax purposes, to divide a single profession into two parts, only one of which is exercised in the UK.[14]

## Foreign partnerships

Where the profession is carried on through a partnership which is controlled and managed abroad by persons who are not resident in the UK, the partnership is considered to be resident abroad, notwithstanding that some of the partners may be resident in the UK.[15] The partnership is chargeable to tax on any profit attributable to that part of the profession exercised in the UK.[16] In addition, a foreign domiciled partner resident in the UK is chargeable to tax on his share of non-UK profits on the remittance basis.

13 TA 1988 s 65.
14 *Davies v Braithwaite* (1933) 18 TC 198, KB.
15 TA 1988 s 112.
16 Ibid s 18(1)(a)(iii).

## Transfer of assets overseas

Performers often think that their tax problems can be resolved by establishing a company or trust outside the UK which either employs them or holds assets on their behalf. Such a course of action is often not effective as there are widely drawn provisions which are designed to prevent the avoidance of income tax by the transfer of income to persons resident or domiciled outside the UK.[17] The legislation provides that where there has been a transfer of assets by an individual, and as a result, directly or indirectly, income is received by a non-resident or non-domiciled individual, company or trust for the direct or indirect benefit, now or in the future, of that individual ordinarily resident in the UK, the Inland Revenue is empowered to apportion the income of the overseas person to the individual provided he has the power to enjoy the income.

Additionally, if assets are transferred in similar circumstances and any individual who is ordinarily resident in the UK received any payment from the overseas person this will be regarded as income.

The effect of these provisions is that it is not generally possible for the performer to avoid a charge to tax on such income unless he is prepared to relinquish his power to enjoy that income. Some planning opportunities do remain in that income producing assets can be transferred for the benefit of other persons with the charge to tax being deferred until monies are applied for their benefit. Any such income is assessed under Schedule D, Case VI and is subject to higher rates of tax.

The provisions will not be invoked if it can be shown that the transactions were for bona fide commercial reasons and were not designed for the purpose of avoiding liability to taxation.

It is beyond the scope of this book to examine all of the anti-avoidance provisions relating to off-shore structures but it may be helpful to set out some guidelines. Overseas arrangements are unlikely to create UK tax savings unless:

(1) the performer is prepared to alienate himself from any benefit of the funds held overseas; or
(2) the performer is prepared to allow the funds to accumulate overseas and accept that tax will ultimately be payable; or
(3) the performer is likely to emigrate from the UK at some future date and is content to allow the funds to accumulate in the meantime.

[17] Ibid s 739.

# 6 Non-resident performers

Non-resident performers are afforded very limited protection under our double taxation agreements and will generally be taxable in the UK on 'live performance' income arising in the UK.

## Withholding tax

A basic rate withholding tax was introduced from 1 May 1987 to assist in the collection of tax which was previously going unpaid. This withholding tax, prima facie, applies to anybody making a payment directly or indirectly connected with a performance in the UK by a non-resident performer whether that performer is employed or self-employed.[1] Residence for this purpose is decided on the basis of domestic law and not by virtue of treaty provisions applying to dual residents. The withholding tax, which is administered by the Inland Revenue's Foreign Entertainers Unit (FEU), is not a tax in its own right but is merely a method of collecting tax on account of the final liability which is calculated in the normal way. The FEU will seek to tax endorsement, sponsorship and merchandising income;[2] it is probably the only tax authority in the world seeking to tax visiting performers on merchandising income.

Withholding may also apply to income and expenses received from activities which involve a political, social, religious or charitable nature if an entertainment character is present. Performers will normally give their services free at such events as charity concerts, for example, but will often receive reimbursement of expenses. Reimbursement in such circumstances will represent a payment to which withholding tax will apply. The provision of air tickets to enable the performer to attend will similarly represent a transfer of value to which withholding should be applied.[3]

Withholding applies to any payment or transfer made in connection with a performance in the UK even if not made directly to the performer.[4] The following payments are specifically excluded:

(1) a payment which is subject to withholding tax under other legislation, eg PAYE;[5]

[1] TA 1988 s 555.
[2] FEU 50 para A2.
[3] IT (Entertainers and Sportsmen) Regulations 1987, SI 1987/530 para 172; FEU 50 para A2.
[4] TA 1988 s 555(2).
[5] SI 1987/530 para 3(3)(a).

(2) a payment made to a person who is resident and ordinarily resident in the UK, who is not connected with or an associate of the performer concerned, and the payment is in respect of services ancillary to the performance of a relevant activity and made at an arm's length price,[6] eg payments for equipment hire and hotel costs;
(3) any payment made to a performer in respect of the proceeds of the sale of records deriving from a sound recording made by the performer.[7]
(4) a payment together with connected payments not exceeding £1,000.[8]

It is not possible to avoid withholding tax by making a payment to a performer by way of a loan which is subsequently forgiven. Where money is loaned to an performer the FEU regard the payment as a connected payment and expect tax to be deducted from the loan.

The term 'transfer' covers the provision of assets to the performer or meeting his pecuniary liabilities. It therefore includes such items as the provision of airline tickets or hotel accommodation as well as payments in kind such as, for example, the prize of a car to a golfer achieving a hole in one at a golf tournament. The cost of the asset transferred in these circumstances is the original cost to the transferor, less so much as has been borne by the performer.[9] This cost is treated as being the net amount of the payment after deduction of basic rate tax and tax must then be accounted for on the basis of the gross value.

## Deduction of tax

The FEU has issued a Payer's Guide FEU 50 (Appendix VII) to help people making payments to non-resident performers. This states that 'any payer who makes a payment, to any person, which arises directly or indirectly from a UK appearance by a non-resident performer must deduct tax at the basic rate'.[10]

The maximum amount of tax which can be withheld from a payment is 25%, even if the performer's eventual tax liability, because he will be liable to tax at the higher 40% rate, will exceed the tax thus deducted.[11]

## Accounting for tax

Whenever a payer withholds tax he must complete a three-part form, the FEU 2, which is broadly similar to a P45. Part 2 is kept by the payer for his own records and Part 3 is given to the payee as a certificate of the payment made and the tax withheld. Part 1 is sent to the Accounts Office, Shipley, on a quarterly basis with the payer's quarterly return of payments made, form FEU 1.[12]

6 Ibid para 3(3)(b).
7 Ibid para 3(3)(c).
8 Ibid para 4(3)(a).
9 Ibid para 17(2)(b).
10 FEU 50 para A1.
11 SI 1987/530 para 4(2).
12 SI 1987/530 para 9(1).

The FEU 1 has to be submitted within 14 days of the return periods ending on 30 June, 30 September, 31 December and 5 April.[13] Any tax due to the Revenue must accompany the FEU 1 and interest and penalties can become payable in the event of late submission of the return. Tax deducted from payments received by the person making the return can be used to 'frank' tax he is required to account for in respect of payments made: tax is only payable to the Revenue if the tax deducted exceeds the tax suffered.[14]

## Reduced withholding applications

Because the amount of withholding would often be excessive if no account were taken of admissible expenses the legislation includes the right to make a reduced withholding application to the FEU.[15]

Unless a reduced withholding tax agreement is reached prior to payment, the payer must withhold tax from the gross payment he makes unless one of the exceptions mentioned above applies.

The application for a reduced withholding tax agreement can be made by any person making or receiving a payment to which withholding applies but it must be made in writing not less than 30 days before the intended payment or transfer.[16] Although it is under no legal obligation to do so, the FEU will in practice accept reduced withholding applications made well within the 30-day time limit if there are bona fide reasons for the late application and the FEU has the resources available to deal with them.

The Payer's Guide sets out the information required in support of a reduced withholding agreement at paragraph B7. This includes dates of arrival in and departure from the UK, whether the performer is likely to return to the UK again before the next 5 April, a projection of income with details of dates and venues, an itemised projection of the expenses which will be incurred and copies of any contracts covering appearances.

In agreeing to a reduced withholding agreement the FEU must at all times aim at securing that the tax payment shall be, as nearly as may be, the amount of liability to tax of the performer or other person arising in relation to the payment after taking into account admissible expenses and higher rate tax liability.[17]

## Groups and teams

If one member of an orchestra is a non-resident performer the FEU will accept that withholding only applies to that performer's salary, not the whole of the box office receipts.

[13] Ibid para 9(2).
[14] Ibid para 4(7).
[15] Ibid para 4(4).
[16] Ibid para 5(1).
[17] Ibid para 4(6)(a).

It may be possible to agree with the FEU that withholding will not normally apply to payments to overseas national sporting boards which bring teams to the UK where the members of the team are their employees. The team members, however, will have a UK tax liability in respect of their salaries and any endorsement etc income earned from their activities in the UK.

The reduced withholding agreement may take into account the fact that the liability has been secured or otherwise provided for whether by a guarantee or other means.[18] In practice the FEU seems very reluctant to enter into guarantee arrangements.

Once an agreement has been reached the FEU will notify all the parties involved in making payments how much tax they are responsible for withholding. If possible the FEU will issue a so-called 'middle-man' agreement to exempt one link in the chain entirely, eg the box-office, on payments to a promoter so that withholding will only apply to payments by the promoter to the performer.

The legislation does not incorporate a right of appeal against the Inland Revenue's decision on a reduced withholding application.

## The basis of charge

Unless the performer is employed and attribution (see below) does not apply, the performer's earnings are treated as received in the course of a separate trade, profession or vocation carried on in the UK by the performer and taxed for each year of assessment on the full amount of the profits or gains arising in that year from payments receivable.[19]

In certain circumstances payments made to third parties will be attributed to and taxed as the income of the performer. Attribution applies where the recipient is:

(1) a person under the control of the performer,[20] for example, his personal service company, or
(2) not resident in the UK and liable to tax in a low tax area (which is defined as meaning an applicable tax rate of 25% or less),[1] or
(3) a settlement of which the performer is settlor,[2] or
(4) a 'stable' company employing numerous performers or a blind trust from which the performer can be expected to benefit.[3]

Attribution will not apply where the performer neither controls the recipient of the connected payment nor can be expected to share directly in that recipient's income. For example, members of an orchestra or circus troupe may be paid a regular salary rather than a fee for each performance. The appropriate part of the salary will be taxable in these circumstances,

18 SI 1987/530 para 4(6)(b).
19 TA 1988 s 556.
20 SI 1987/530 para 7(2)(a).
1 Ibid para 7(2)(b).
2 Ibid para 7(2)(c).
3 Ibid para 7(2)(d).

not a proportion of the overall fee paid to the orchestra or profit arising to the circus owner.

As treaty law overrules domestic legislation it follows that attribution can only apply where the performer is resident in a country which either has no double taxation agreement with the UK or which has a treaty with the UK which includes the equivalent of article 17(2) of the OECD model treaty - see Appendix IX.

The normal rules for computing profits under Cases I and II of Schedule D apply except that expenses incurred by a person other than a performer may be allowed, on a just and reasonable basis, in computing those profits.[4]

Any person who has received a payment or transfer under deduction of tax or to whom a tax liability is treated as arising, may make a claim in writing that the tax payment made was excessive. The normal appeal provisions apply in these circumstances to the Inspector's decision on such a claim. The claim cannot be made before the end of the relevant tax year but can be made within six years of the end of the year in which the connected payment or transfer was made.[5]

## Expenses

### FEU scale of allowable expenses

To facilitate the processing of reduced withholding agreements the FEU drew up guidelines of acceptable levels of expenses for internal use. The FEU stressed in 1989 that actual expenditure would be allowed, 'provided there was no question of private benefit'.

### Travel expenses to and from the UK

From 1991 the FEU has agreed that there is no need to apportion international travel costs where the performer comes to the UK for an activity and returns directly to his home base as long as the travel is for business purposes only. In other cases, eg where the performer flies to the UK from another engagement, the amount allowable is subject to negotiation.

### Allocation of income and expenditure

Disputes can arise with the FEU regarding the allocation of expenses between UK and non-UK activities, eg where those expenses are incurred for the purposes of a European or world tour by a musician. A proportion of pre-production, rehearsal, set design and construction costs can all be claimed as admissible and the method of apportionment will need to be agreed with the FEU, often on the basis of the number of dates in the tour. Where the UK element of expenditure is readily identifiable, however,

[4] SI 1987/530 para 8.
[5] Ibid para 13.

the FEU will expect that to be used rather than a proportion of the total expenditure. The FEU is reluctant to allow a proportion of a performer's office overhead as a deduction in computing the UK tax liability.

A film actor's contract will usually only cover principal photography although the actor will often be involved in other activities in relation to the film, such as role research, rehearsals and promotion once the film is completed. The FEU will resist the allocation of part of an actor's fee to these other activities where the contract states that the whole of the fee is for principal photography. The FEU will also argue that certain duties are more valuable than others and is unlikely to accept a straight allocation of a fee on a time basis.

## Planning

It should be noted that the special rules treating the performer's activity as a separate trade taxable on the arising basis only apply if the performer is not resident in the UK for the year in question. If the performer is resident in the UK for the relevant year then the normal basis of assessment will apply, ie the preceding year basis[6] even if the performer has not previously been to the UK. Accordingly, he will be taxed on the basis of the profits earned on his accounting period ended in the preceding fiscal year (assuming the profession commenced before 6 April 1994). If the earnings for that period were significantly lower than those earned in the UK it can be advantageous to ensure that the performer becomes UK resident.

6 TA 1988 s 60 (prior to amendment by FA 1994).

# 7 Value added tax

It is not the intention of this book to examine in depth the workings of value added tax (VAT). There are, however, a number of areas where VAT does have an impact on the affairs of performers.

## Registration, returns and control visits

If a performer is receiving income in excess of £45,000 pa he will need to register for VAT.[1] It should be noted that where there is a partnership of performers, eg a rock group, this limitation applies to the partnership activities as a whole. It is important that the requirement to register for VAT is recognised as severe penalties (of 30% of the tax) can be levied.[2] The requirement to register arises if a performer's supplies in the previous 12 months have exceeded £45,000 or if he expects his supplies in the next 30 days to exceed £45,000.[3]

Once registered, quarterly returns must be submitted to Customs and Excise within 30 days of the end of the quarter and any tax due paid within the same time limit.[4] If these time limits are not adhered to a default surcharge or penalty of up to 15% of the tax charged for the period covered by the return may be made.[5]

If returns are completed incorrectly there is also the risk of incurring a serious misdeclaration penalty of up to 15%.[6]

Customs and Excise have available and use very wide powers in relation to VAT, the local VAT office having prime responsibility for the collection of the correct amount of tax. One of their principal activities is therefore to make 'control visits' to business premises and inspect the records.

## Records

In order to enable Customs and Excise to make these checks on VAT returns, certain VAT accounting rules must be complied with.

1 VATA 1983 Sch 1 para (1)(a).
2 FA 1985 s 15.
3 VATA 1983 Sch 1 para (1)(b).
4 VAT (General) Regulations 1985 SI 1985/886 para 58.
5 FA 1985 s 19.
6 Ibid s 14.

A performer need not keep his records and accounts in any particular form, but they must contain sufficient information to enable him to calculate his output and input tax correctly and to complete the necessary returns.[7] They must therefore contain details of all income and expenditure whether fully taxable, exempt, or zero-rated.

Tax invoices and all supporting documentation and accounts in respect of income and expenditure must be retained to support the returns and filed in order, so that the returns can be checked against them.

A specific requirement is that a performer must have a VAT account to show the net liability (or repayment) due for each return period.[8] An analysed cash book or day book must also be kept to provide a link between invoices and the VAT account. All VAT related records must be retained for six years.[9] In general, Customs and Excise normally accept computerised VAT records. If a business is considering installing or amending its computer system it is necessary to consult Customs and Excise in advance to confirm that they find the system acceptable for VAT purposes.

## Supply

### United Kingdom

VAT is generally chargeable whenever goods or services are supplied in the UK.[10] Anything done for a consideration which is not a supply of goods is treated as a supply of services.[11] Wages and salaries are not subject to VAT so a performer who is directly employed will not charge VAT. Supplies by a self-employed UK performer or his UK company will prime facie be taxable.

The supply of cultural, sporting or entertainment services outside the UK are outside the scope of UK VAT[12] but may be subject to overseas VAT or equivalent local sales taxes (see below). The UK organiser of a performance overseas (such as a booking agent) is subject to a potentially complex VAT regime according to where the performance takes place.

Where the performance takes place outside the EC no UK VAT should be charged on agent's commission.

If the performance is inside the EC and the performer is UK VAT registered the agent should charge UK VAT on his commission. Where the performer is VAT registered elsewhere in the EC and provides a VAT registration number, UK VAT is not chargeable on the agent's commission. Where the performer is not VAT registered in the EC the agent is required to register for VAT in the country of performance and charge local VAT on his commission.

A non-UK performer coming to the UK for a one-off engagement or a short tour who does not establish an office in the UK will, from November

7 VATA 1983 Sch 7 para 1.
8 C & E Notice 700 para 64.
9 VATA 1983 Sch 7 para 2.
10 Ibid s 1.
11 Ibid s 3(2)(b).
12 VAT (Place of Supply of Services) Order 1992 SI 1992/3121 para 15(a), (c).

1993, not be required to register in the UK. Instead the VAT on his supplies is dealt with by the recipient of those supplies under the 'reverse-charge' procedure.[13]

**Outside the UK**

The entertainer or sportsman performing outside his home territory may find that he is required to register for VAT or equivalent local sales taxes. A summary of the position in the major territories is below:

*European Community (EC)*

The 12 EC nations operate very similar VAT regimes in respect of non-resident entertainers or sportsmen performing in their territories. Under EC directives the supply for VAT purposes is deemed to take place in the country of performance and it is in that territory that VAT must be accounted for.

All of the EC countries with the exceptions of Ireland and Luxembourg operate 'VAT Shift' rules enabling the performer's VAT liability to be accounted for by the promoter or organiser of the event. Belgium permits the VAT shift for one-off appearances or relatively short term engagements.

Appendix XII provides a summary of the position in the EC.

All EC territories operate VAT reclaim schemes for non-residents. Claims must be submitted by the 30 June following the calendar year in which the VAT was incurred.

*Other European non-EC Countries*

Many of these operate similar VAT regimes to the EC members (eg Austria and Hungary). Some territories do not currently have VAT systems (eg Switzerland).

It is recommended that local professional advice is taken before finalising contracts for these territories.

*Other territories*

It would be difficult to provide a full summary of the many different VAT regimes, however the position in some of the major territories is as follows:

*Australia*

No requirement to register for sales tax.

13 VATA 1983 Sch 4 Item 8.

*Canada*

Registration for goods and service tax (GST) may be necessary if the non-resident is regarded as carrying on commercial activities. Local advice should be taken.

*Japan*

The services of non-resident entertainers and sportsmen will be subject to consumption tax at a current rate of 3%. The collection and payment of this will normally be dealt with by the local promoter.

*New Zealand*

Registration for goods and service tax (GST) is only required where a permanent place of business is established in New Zealand.

*United States*

Non-resident entertainers and sportsmen do not need to register for sales tax in the US.

## Royalties

Where there is an obligation to pay royalties this derives from the transfer or assignment of a copyright or from the granting of a licence to use a copyright.

This is regarded as a supply of services but is outside the scope of VAT if made to:

(1) a person who belongs in a country outside the EEC or Isle of Man; or
(2) a person who belongs in another EEC state and who receives the supply for business purposes and is registered for VAT in that EEC state.[14]

For VAT purposes, each payment of the royalty is regarded as a separate supply taking place on the earlier of payment being received or an invoice being issued.[15]

## Entry and similar fees

Entry fees to competitions involving sport or physical recreation where the whole of the entry fee is returned as prizes or where the competition is organised by a non-profit making body established for sporting purposes are exempt from VAT.[16]

[14] SI 1992/3121 para 16.
[15] SI 1985/886 para 24.
[16] VATA 1983 Sch 6 Group 10.

The VAT exemption for sports services is unlikely to apply to performers since it is only available where the supply is made by a non-profit making body.[17]

## Player transfers

Where a sports club transfers a player to another club, this constitutes a supply of services, namely a supply of staff, and is thus subject to VAT. VAT does not normally, however, apply to sums paid either to the player himself by way of a signing-on fee or to the governing body by way of levy since these fall outside the scope of VAT. Where a player is transferred from a UK club to a foreign club, the transfer fee will be outside the scope of VAT.[18]

## Sponsorship

Sponsorship should be distinguished from true donations for VAT purposes as noted on p 35. The performer is usually doing something for the benefit of the sponsor, eg providing publicity and receiving sponsorship income as consideration. The performer is therefore making a taxable supply. He must charge tax and issue a VAT invoice to the sponsor in respect of the transaction if the performer is registered for VAT. The value on which tax must be charged is the amount excluding the VAT itself which the sponsor has agreed to pay. Where, however, a fee has been agreed without reference to VAT, and a tax invoice is not issued adding the VAT to the agreed fee, then the amount agreed should be treated as tax inclusive.

On the other hand true donations are outside the scope of VAT. In such cases the donor receives nothing in exchange from the performer and there is often no written agreement. True donations can sometimes occur, eg in connection with testimonials and benefits for sportsmen.

It is important that the performer recognises a sponsorship receipt on which he should charge VAT since the responsibility to account for VAT is his even if he fails to charge it.

Where a sponsor is based in a different country to that of the recipient, the fee will normally be outside the scope of UK VAT but VAT will be accounted for by the sponsor under the 'reverse charge' provisions.

## Planning

Performers can take advantage of some general VAT planning techniques:

- maximising recovery of input tax;
- recovery of input tax at the earliest opportunity;

[17] VAT (Sport, Physical Education and Fund Raising Events) Order 1994.
[18] SI 1992/3121 para 16.

- postponing payment of output tax to Customs and Excise within permitted limits.

The first results in the saving of tax, the latter two in a cash flow benefit. Some examples are:

- reclaiming VAT on purchases made prior to registration where permitted;
- analysing business activities into individual transactions and only charging VAT where appropriate;
- invoicing at the beginning of a return period rather than at the end of the previous period to defer payment of output tax to Customs and Excise;
- claiming at least a portion of expenditure which has a dual purpose, ie business and private elements;
- if turnover is less than £300,000 opting to apply VAT on a cash basis rather than the normal accruals basis.

# 8 National Insurance

National Insurance contributions (NIC) are generally payable by all persons working in the United Kingdom. The liability and type of contribution is dependent upon whether a performer is self-employed or employed.

As with tax legislation, it is not always clear whether any particular individual is employed or self-employed and his status will depend on the facts of his particular case. The principles are broadly similar to those for tax set out on p 19 but there can occasionally be differences.[1] The Inland Revenue and Contributions Agency will now liaise to ensure consistent treatment.

Tax relief is not available for National Insurance contributions except those paid as an employer and Class 4 contributions (see below).

## Self-employed

Those individuals who are self-employed are required to pay contributions of two types, Class 2 and Class 4.

### Class 2 contributions

These contributions are payable at the rate of £5.65 per week where earnings exceed £3,200 per tax year.[2]

### Class 4 contributions

These are payable in addition to Class 2 contributions and are calculated on the individual's taxable profits. The rate of contributions is 7.3% on profits between £6,490 and £22,360.[3] The maximum amount payable is £1,158.51. The contributions are collected by the Inland Revenue at the same time as income tax under Schedule D, Cases I and II.

One half of the contribution payable for a year of assessment can be deducted when calculating taxable profits.[4]

1 NI 39.
2 SSCBA 1992 s 11.
3 Ibid s 15.
4 ICTA 1988 s 617(5).

## Employees

Performers who are employed are required to pay Class 1 primary contributions. The rates of contribution are set out in the table below and will depend on whether the employer provides a pension scheme which is contracted out of the earnings-related State scheme.[5]

In addition to the employee's contributions, the employer is also required to pay secondary Class 1 contributions.[5]

### National Insurance contributions

| *Class 1* | *Not contracted out* | | *Contracted out* | |
|---|---|---|---|---|
| EMPLOYEES | | | | |
| *Earnings per week* | *On first £57 pw* | *On excess to £430 pw* | *On first £57 pw* | *On excess to £430 pw* |
| £0–£56.99 | – | – | – | – |
| £57–£430 | 2% | 10% | 2% | 8.2% |
| Over £430 | £38.44 pw | £31.72 pw | | |

| EMPLOYERS | | | |
|---|---|---|---|
| *Earnings per week* | *Rate applied to all earnings* | *On first £57 pw* | *On excess to £430 pw* |
| £0–£56.99 | – | – | – |
| £57–£99.99 | 3.6% | 3.6% | 0.6% |
| £100–£144.99 | 5.6% | 5.6% | 2.6% |
| £145–£199.99 | 7.6% | 7.6% | 4.6% |
| £200–£430.00 | 10.2% | 10.2% | 7.2% |
| Over £430 | 10.2% | £32.67 plus 10.2% on earnings in excess of £430 pw | |

Employers are also required to account for NIC on scale charges for cars and fuel supplied to employees.[6] Contributions are collected through the PAYE system.

### *Annual maximum*

Where a performer is employed in more than one employment or is both employed and self-employed then his liability for primary Class 1 and Class 2 contributions for any tax year is not to exceed an amount equal to 53 primary Class 1 contributions at the standard rate, ie £1,998.88 for 1994/95.[7]

Where a performer is both employed and self employed then his liability for Class 4 contributions for that year is not to exceed an amount equal to 53 times the Class 2 contributions payable for the year plus the amount of Class 4 contributions payable on the upper annual limit for Class 4

5 SSCBA 1992 s 6.
6 SSCBA 1992 s 10.
7 Social Security (Contributions) Regulations 1979, SI 1979/591 para 17(1).

less the Class 1 primary and Class 2 contributions actually payable by him. For 1994 the upper limit would normally be £1,457.96 (ie 53 × £5.65 + £1,158.51).[8]

### *Deferment*

Where a performer is both employed and self-employed during a year and is likely to pay excess contributions he can apply to the DSS for a certificate of deferment in respect of the Class 2 and Class 4 liabilities.[9] This can be done by submitting form CF359 to the Deferment Group of the DSS at Newcastle-upon-Tyne, NE98 1YU.

## Planning

The imposition of the 10.2% employer's contribution rate on all earnings has a significant impact on the use of employment companies for performers. The effect of the charge is illustrated on p 50 and if it is not expected that significant amounts of time are to be spent overseas, it may be preferable to opt for self-employed status if possible. Where employment is preferred or unavoidable, the effect of the NIC charge should be mitigated where possible. The NIC charge generally only applies to 'cash' remuneration and therefore the following types of benefit may not attract NIC:

(1) cheap or interest-free loans;
(2) contributions to pension schemes;
(3) vouchers but not vouchers for cash;
(4) accommodation;
(5) other assets (excluding certain shares, financial instruments, commodities and insurance policies).

Consideration could also be given to the use of a non-resident company without a place of business in the UK as an employer for duties performed outside the UK as such an employer would not be required to account for NIC.

Despite anti-avoidance measures there are still ways of awarding bonuses in kind and avoiding employer's NIC at 10.2%. These are likely to continue unchanged for the moment and include the use of vouchers and certain investments and in view of the potential saving are well worth considering.

Where a performer is not a director of the company employing him it may be possible to mitigate the employee NIC contributions. Where an individual is paid on a weekly or monthly basis the pay period for NIC purposes is taken on a weekly or monthly basis.

Where the pay for a particular pay period exceeds the limit for NIC purposes, any excess is not charged to NIC. Accordingly, the payment of bonuses can be made intermittently without attracting a charge to employees' NIC.

[8] SI 1979/591 para 67(1).
[9] Ibid paras 54A(1), 63.

## International aspects

The rate of social security contribution in many European countries is significantly higher than in the UK. Where performers move to and work in other countries the social security aspects are therefore well worth consideration. In particular, planning prior to taking up a foreign assignment or prior to arrival in the UK is necessary to:

- avoid double liability to contributions;
- ensure that appropriate credit is given for contributions payable;
- protect existing benefits by making voluntary contributions where appropriate;
- make arrangements for medical cover.

As regards the UK, Class 2 contributions remain payable while temporarily working outside Great Britain, while on holiday or resting. There is no liability to Class 4 contributions for any year in which the performer is not resident in the UK. Where the performer is resident for part of the year there is Class 4 liability for the whole year.

The planning process requires an understanding of local social security legislation, the terms of reciprocal or other agreements with the UK, the special rules relating to cross border working within the EC (where applicable) and the administrative procedures adopted by the DHSS and overseas social security authorities.

Many countries require non-resident entertainers or sportsmen performing in their territory to pay social security contributions and this is usually enforced by deduction at source. Fortunately, there are bilateral social security treaties between many countries which allow these deductions to be avoided. In order to be covered by the treaty the entertainer or sportsman must be within the scope of the social security laws of his or her home country.

Exemption in the country of performance is normally secured by presenting a certificate issued by the home country authorities.

With effect from 1 January 1994 five EFTA states have joined the EC rules for social security. These countries are Austria, Finland, Iceland, Norway and Sweden. In general, for activities commencing after that date, the EC rules will apply rather than the terms of a bilateral treaty. For example within the European Union UK residents may obtain a certificate, form E101, from:

Department of Social Security (DSS)
Overseas Branch
Newcastle Upon Tyne
NE98 1YX

The DSS will require the following information:

Full name and address
Maiden name (if appropriate)
Date of birth
Nationality
National insurance number

Details of the overseas engagement

US residents can obtain certification from:

Social Security Administration
OIO - Totalisation
Post Office Box 17049
Baltimore
Maryland 21235
USA

# Appendices

# Appendix I
# Sports Aid Foundation checklist

**Sports Aid Foundation**

## Athletes and Taxation

**Touche Ross**

The Inland Revenue has taken particular interest in the taxation of sportsmen and sportswomen over recent years specifically through the Special Offices. There is also a worrying lack of awareness by sportsmen and sportswomen about their tax obligations. If you are able to answer yes to the following questions, the chances are you will be able to avoid problems with the taxman.

1. **Is the Inland Revenue aware of your income from sport?**

   *Even if you have no tax to pay because your income is not sufficiently large at the moment later problems can often be avoided by making your local Inspector aware of your sports activities.*

2. **Do you keep details of your income from sport including sponsorship, personal appearance money (not only at sports events) and payments in kind?**

   *The Inland Revenue may ask you for this information and check it against information they obtain from other sources e.g. press clippings.*

3. **Do you keep details of your expenses such as travelling, training etc?**

   *You may be asked to show that your expenses exceed your income and so demonstrate that there is no taxable profit from your activities; alternatively these expenses may help you reduce any taxable profit.*

4. **Does your income from sport each year exceed your expenses and if so have you advised your Inspector of Taxes?**

   *It is your responsibility to tell the Inland Revenue if you have taxable profits, not for the Inspector to ask you. Failure to do so will render you liable to penalties.*

5. **Do you have a Trust Fund and keep details and payments in and out of it?**

   *Income paid into such a fund is subject to tax whether or not it is paid out to you.*

6. **Have you put any money aside to meet your tax liabilities?**

   *If you can't pay on time the Inland Revenue may take action against you personally to recover the tax and will certainly charge you interest.*

7. **Do you know what happens when you earn income from abroad?**

   *You will pay UK income tax on such income and may have a liability to foreign tax – this is a complex area where you need specialist advice.*

8. **Have you considered putting money away in order to save tax?**

   *There are a number of investments which have tax benefits e.g. pensions which are well worth considering.*

9. **Does your annual income from the sport exceed £37,600 p.a?**

   *You will probably need to be registered for value added tax purposes.*

If you are unable to answer most of the above questions and think that your income may very well exceed your expenses you need to consider your tax position **as a matter of urgency.** If your expenses (reduced by SAF grants) are likely to exceed your income then you can probably relax, provided that you have the details to prove this to the Inland Revenue's satisfaction. If you don't know then you should produce some figures **urgently**.

I shall be very happy to answer any questions which this note may prompt.

*Richard Baldwin, Touche Ross & Co., Hill House, 1 Little New Street, London EC4A 3TR.*

*Telephone No: 071-936-3000.*

September 1993

Note: the figure in paragraph 9 above has been increased to £45,000 pa.

# Appendix II
# Cash flow statement

This statement is designed to develop basic information relating to cash income and expenditure over the next 12 to 24 months as an aid to the financial planning process and can be used to develop a personal cash flow forecast.

## 1 Cash income

| | *Current year* | | *Future year* | |
|---|---|---|---|---|
| Income from performer's activities: | | | | |
| | £ | £ | £ | £ |
| Salary (net) | | | | |
| Bonuses | | | | |
| Profits/drawings | | | | |
| Other (specify) | | | | |
| Income from other sources: | | | | |
| Dividends (net) | | | | |
| Interest | | | | |
| Other (specify) | | | | |
| | | | | |
| Net proceeds from sale of | | | | |
| assets (specify): | | | | |
| | | | | |

| | *Current year* | | *Future year* | |
|---|---|---|---|---|
| Less: Tax paid in year | | | | |
| | £ | £ | £ | £ |
| Income tax* | | | | |
| National insurance* | | | | |
| CGT | | | | |
| CTT/inheritance tax | | | | |
| | | | | |
| After-tax income | | | | |

*Do not include tax deducted at source (eg PAYE or tax credits on dividends).

## 2 Annual recurring expenditure

| | *Current year* | | *Future year* | |
|---|---|---|---|---|
| | £ | £ | £ | £ |
| Mortgage payments (rent) | | | | |
| Light/heat/telephone | | | | |
| Maintenance | | | | |
| Furniture & equipment | | | | |
| Rates | | | | |
| Domestic help | | | | |
| Insurance | | | | |
| Other (specify) | | | | |
| | | | | |
| Living: | | | | |
| Food & household expenses | | | | |
| Clothing | | | | |
| Medical care | | | | |
| Travel to work | | | | |
| Car expenses | | | | |
| Children | | | | |
| Education | | | | |
| Pocket money/allowances | | | | |
| Other (specify) | | | | |

| | *Current year* | | *Future year* | |
|---|---|---|---|---|
| Miscellaneous: | | | | |
| | £ | £ | £ | £ |
| Maintenance | | | | |
| Entertainment | | | | |
| Recreation | | | | |
| Loan & credit card payments | | | | |
| Personal pension premiums | | | | |
| Life assurance premiums | | | | |
| Interest on overdrafts | | | | |
| Interest on loans etc | | | | |
| Debt repayment | | | | |
| Holidays | | | | |
| Deeds of covenant: | | | | |
| • charitable | | | | |
| • other | | | | |
| Regular savings | | | | |
| Other (specify) | | | | |
| Total basic recurring expenditure | | | | |
| Non-recurring major expenditure: | | | | |
| Investments | | | | |
| Capital acquisitions | | | | |
| Medical bills | | | | |
| Other (specify) | | | | |
| Total expenses | | | | |
| Net cash income/deficit | | | | |

# Appendix III
# Tax-favoured investments

| *Item* | *Tax benefit* | *Comment* |
|---|---|---|
| National Savings Certificates | Growth in value is completely free of all taxes. Index-linked issues are available. | Maximum investment in each issue is £10,000 per holder. |
| National Savings yearly plan | Growth in value is completely free of all taxes. | Maximum investment is £400 per month per holder. |
| National Savings Bank ordinary and investment accounts | Interest on ordinary accounts is tax-free up to £70 per year. (£140 for husband and wife jointly.) | Larger deposits are permitted, but interest exceeding £70 is taxable. Interest is paid gross, unlike other bank deposit interest. |
| Premium bonds | Winnings are tax-free. | Maximum investment is £20,000 per holder. |
| Save As You Earn (building societies) | Growth in value is completely free of all taxes. | Maximum investment is £20 per month over five years. Tax-free bonuses paid after five or seven years. |
| Government securities and qualifying corporate bonds | No capital gains tax. | Low coupon can be matched with high capital gain or vice versa. |
| Tax Exempt Special Savings Accounts | Interest earning accounts which are free of tax. | Initial deposit must be invested for five years. Maximum investment of £9,000. First year £3,000 and £1,800 pa subsequently until total reached. |

| *Item* | *Tax benefit* | *Comment* |
|---|---|---|
| Pensions | Investment in company pension scheme, personal pension scheme or retirement annuity scheme is tax deductible up to certain limits (see Chapter 4). Tax-free lump sums and/or annuity are payable on retirement. | Income and gains in the pension fund are tax-free, so the investment returns are higher. |
| Principal private residence | Gain exempt from capital gains tax. | Interest on loan of up to £30,000 for purchase qualifies for 20% tax relief (15% 1995/96). |
| Furnished holiday lettings | Losses may be set off against general income. Gains can be deferred if proceeds reinvested. | Provided detailed conditions are satisfied the activity is treated as a trade. |
| Enterprise Investment Scheme | Investment by subscription for shares in unquoted companies qualifies for tax relief at 20%. Relief for losses on disposal is given against either capital gains or income. Capital gains are tax free. | There are complex conditions. Amount qualifying for tax relief limited to £100,000 pa. |
| Personal equity plan | Income and capital gains from investment can be tax-free. | Maximum investment £6,000 pa in a general PEP. £3,000 pa in a single company PEP. |
| Life assurance | Proceeds in policyholder's hands free of income and capital gains tax. | The policy must be a qualifying policy and usually must be held for 10 years for full tax exemption. |

| *Item* | *Tax benefit* | *Comment* |
|---|---|---|
| Leasing commercial buildings | Purchase price (excluding land) qualifies for tax allowances which may be offset against other income. | 100% tax allowance for commercial buildings in enterprise zones. Tax conditions complex and quality of investment important. |

It should be noted that the first £5,800 of chargeable capital gains from the disposal of chargeable assets (eg stocks and shares), in each tax year, is ignored for capital gains tax purposes.

No specific recommendation is made in respect of any of the above investments and advice shall be taken from a professional investment adviser before taking any investment decision.

# Appendix IV The use of a captive employer company

The following is a summary of the main tax and commercial points to be considered when deciding whether the performer's activities should be structured as a company or as a self-employed performer in business on his own or in partnership. In the case of a company the performer would normally be appointed a director drawing his remuneration as director's fees whereas under the alternative his earnings would be taken as business or partnership drawings.

## Tax factors

| *Sole performer/partnership* | *Company* |
|---|---|
| Date for payment of tax | |
| The 'preceding-year' basis of assessment can mean up to 20 or 26 months' delay between earning profits and payment of the tax on them. Following the change in rules this will fall to 9 to 15 months. | Tax is generally payable nine months after the profits are earned. Advance corporation tax (ACT) on a dividend at the rate of 20/80 currently due 14 days after the end of the calendar quarter in which the dividend is paid. |
| Drawings | |
| Money can be drawn out of the business without any immediate tax cost. Income is taxed directly on the performer(s). If after-tax profit is left in the business, it can be drawn out tax-free at any time. | Any money taken out of the business (usually in the form of salary, director's fees, rent, dividends etc) attracts a current income tax liability even if the company has made a tax loss. |
| Losses | |
| A tax loss made by the business can be set against the performer's other income (in some cases for earlier years) thereby obtaining tax relief at an early date. | A tax loss within a company cannot be set against the performer's other income for tax purposes, although a loss suffered on the disposal of shares in an unquoted trading company can, subject to certain conditions, be set off against the taxpayer's general income. |

| *Sole performer/partnership* | *Company* |
|---|---|
| Incorporation/disincorporation | |
| The business can usually be incorporated without tax complications. | It is difficult and costly in tax terms to disincorporate a company. |
| Basis of assessment | |
| The use of the first year's trading results for two or three years' tax assessments can mean obtaining a tax deduction two/three times for allowable expenditure incurred in the initial year. (The corollary of this is that income earned in the initial period may be taxed two/three times). In addition, the commencement and cessation provisions can result in certain income escaping taxation. This advantage will disappear under the new rules for the taxation of the self-employed. | Each year stands on its own with income and expenses being included once only.<br>There are no special assessment provisions at commencement or cessation. |
| Deferral of taxation | |
| Taxable trading income is taxable at normal graduated rates of income tax directly on the performer/partners (maximum rate 40%). The fact that the income may not be drawn out does not affect the position, ie there is no deferral of tax. | The small companies tax rate of 25% is available on the first £300,000 of taxable trading income. This may be the maximum exposure to tax for many years, if low salaries and dividends are paid. At some future date, capital gains tax on the shares may be payable. |
| Notional distributions | |
| Partnership income is taxed directly on the partners. | There is no current taxation on the performer(s) assuming no salary etc. |
| Splitting the assessment | |
| Profits can be attributed to a performer's wife with consequent use of her personal allowances and own tax bands providing she is a partner and 'personally acting' in the partnership. | It may be difficult to secure a deduction for more than a nominal salary to the wife of a director/shareholder unless she works full time in the business. |

| *Sole performer/partnership* | *Company* |
|---|---|
| Deductible expenses | |
| Expenses incurred 'wholly and exclusively' for the purposes of the trade are deductible. | Expenses incurred 'wholly and exclusively' for the purposes of the company's trade are deductible, but if the expenses benefit the directors, a taxable benefit in kind may arise on which the directors will have to pay income tax unless the expense was incurred 'wholly, exclusively and necessarily' for the purposes of the director's employment. |
| Compensation payments to performers | |
| Such payments would usually be treated as additional payments for goodwill and subject to capital gains tax. They are not tax deductible. | The first £30,000 of bona fide termination payments is tax free. Payments are tax deductible subject to normal rules. |
| Pensions | |
| Contributions to finance personal pension plans are deductible up to limits set out on p 66. | Self-administered directors' pension schemes are possible. There is no limit on the deductibility of the company's contributions but the maximum Inland Revenue-approved benefits must not be exceeded. |
| Parallel loans back to the performer/partners are possible from the life company. | A direct loan back of up to 50% of a self-administered fund to the company is possible (other than in the early years) and investment in property for the use of the company is allowed. |
| Annuities to retired partners are deductible and count as earned income up to certain limits. They can be index-linked. | Pensions paid to retired directors are deductible if reasonable. |
| Foreign income | |
| The UK resident partners in a partnership controlled and managed abroad are fully taxable on their non-UK source income from the partnership. | Foreign income of a non-UK resident company, owned by UK resident shareholders, is not taxable on the company, but anti-avoidance provisions would normally apply to the shareholders, rendering the company's income fully subject to UK tax in their hands. |

| *Sole performer/partnership* | *Company* |
|---|---|
| Loss carry-back | |
| Losses in the first four years can be carried back three years against other income. | Losses can be carried back three years but only against the company's profits and not that of the shareholder. |
| Loan interest relief | |
| Interest relief applies even if the partner has less than a 5% interest. | No interest relief is given unless the company is a close trading company and the shareholder has at least 5% of the share capital (or he owns less than 5% but works for the greater part of his time in the management of the business). |
| Capital gains tax (CGT) | |
| CGT is payable by partners on their proportionate share of a capital gain on a partnership asset. No further tax arises thereafter. There is an annual exemption for each individual. | A 'double charge' to CGT may arise, once when an asset is sold by the company and again when the shares in the company (enhanced in value by the after-tax gain) are sold or the company is liquidated. There is no annual exemption for gains for a company. |
| Trading losses of a partnership can be set off against individual capital gains. | Current trading losses of a company may be set off against current capital gains. |
| Capital gains tax roll-over relief | |
| Relief is available on the sale of the partnership business and certain assets (including goodwill) and extends to assets owned by the partner personally but used rent-free in the trade. Relief is available as long as the proceeds are reinvested in 'new' assets (including those of a new trade) within three years after, or one year before, disposal. | Relief is available on the sale of certain assets by a company in the same way as for an unincorporated business. Relief is available in limited circumstances on the disposal of shares where there is reinvestment in the share capital of certain types of company. |
| Capital gains tax – relief for gifts | |
| Individuals (including partners in a partnership) may be able to give away assets on a CGT deferred basis ('hold over' relief). The donee takes on the cost basis of the donor. The objective is to facilitate lifetime gifting for inheritance tax purposes. | The relief is not available to companies as such, but individuals owning shares in companies may give them away on a CGT deferred basis as described opposite. |

| *Sole performer/partnership* | *Company* |
|---|---|
| Introduction of new partner/shareholder | |
| The introduction of a new partner of the departure of an old one creates a new partnership and therefore triggers a cessation of trade for tax purposes unless all the partners before and after elect for a continuance (see p 32). The consequences of a discontinuance are normally severe if profits are rising, so an election is usually made. This will change under the new rules for the self-employed. | A change in shareholders does not affect the continuity of the company. The sale of shares in a company to an incoming investor attracts CGT on the vendor. The gifting of shares to avoid the individual paying CGT may have either inheritance tax consequences or possibly be assessed on the recipient as a benefit in kind. A change of ownership of more than 50% of the shares in a company may result in losses and ACT not being carried forward. |
| If the assets (including goodwill) of a partnership or sole performer are gifted or transferred to an undervalue either to an existing 'connected' partner or to a third party, CGT may be payable. | |
| If the incoming partner pays for goodwill, all the partners are treated as disposing of a fraction of their goodwill and CGT may be payable. In practice, most new partners do not pay for goodwill except by working for the partnership and as long as the new partners and the old are not connected (except as partners) the Inland Revenue does not, in practice, treat a change as a disposal of goodwill. The same applies to a mere change in profit-sharing ratios. If, however, capital assets are revalued and allocated to capital shares through the accounts, CGT may be payable. | |
| National Insurance | |
| Class 2 and 4 contributions payable (see Chapter 8). | Class 1 contributions payable by company and performer (see Chapter 8). |
| Personal liability of performer | |
| Total, joint and several in the case of partnership. | Limited to share capital contributed. In practice, limited liability is partially lost by personal bank guarantees. |

| *Sole performer/partnership* | *Company* |
|---|---|
| Nature of entity | |
| A partnership is not a separate legal entity in England (though it is in Scotland). A 'firm' cannot own property, but a partner may bind all the other partners. | A company is a separate body with an existence regardless of any change in its shareholders or directors. It may contract in its own corporate name as long as the contract is within the scope of its articles of association. If it is not, the directors or shareholders may be personally liable. |
| Membership | |
| The maximum is 20 partners. | Minimum of one shareholder. |
| Loans to performers | |
| As agreed by the partners. Such loans are generally free of tax. | Loans in general are prohibited if the performer is a director. A deposit of 'notional' ACT is required until the loan is repaid. |
| Withdrawal of capital | |
| As agreed by partners. | Restricted by company law. |
| Audit | |
| As agreed by partners. | Required by company law. |
| Privacy | |
| No public filing of accounts required. | Accounts have to be filed with the Registrar of Companies. |
| Access to capital | |
| Only from partners or banks etc. | Access to financial markets. |
| Management | |
| As agreed by the partners. This can lead to disputes as to management methods etc. | Ownership can be separated from management, eg by appointment of a managing director who is not a shareholder. |
| Compliance costs | |
| Minimal filing tax returns. | Audit tax and other registration of compliance fees tend to be more substantial. |

# Appendix V
# Income tax return of payment for services or in respect of a copyright

**Income Tax** **Return of payments for services or a copyright**

*For official use only*

Issued by ____________________________ Payer's District

**Note** *If there is any query on this form please get in touch with the District shown above* ***not the payer***

1. Payee's name and address ____________________________

2. Stage name ____________________________

3. Name of artist, production, act, group etc *where not payee's name* ____________________________

4. Gross amount of payments including expenses payments £ ____________

   Payments include VAT ☐ exclude VAT ☐ *'√' one box*

   For the period from ____________ to ____________

5. Description of services ____________________________

6. Payee's National Insurance number *where known* ____________

7. Description of any other valuable consideration ____________

   *If you need more space please use the back of this form*

8. Payer's name ____________ date ____________

**46R-1**

6728/1124L Dd 8098125 220M 1/89 TP Gp607

**Details of any other valuable consideration**

# Appendix VI Inland Revenue form P11D (1993)

Inland Revenue

For official use
Assessing point reference
if elsewhere

Employer's name ______________ PAYE reference ______________

Director's/employee's* name ______________ NI number [ | | | | ]

*delete as appropriate

**Return of expenses payments and benefits etc not covered by a dispensation - directors, and employees earning at a rate of £8,500 a year or more.**
**Year ended 5 April 1994**
You are required to make this return by 6 June 1994 and to complete and send form P11D(b) to the Inspector.
Please read forms P11D(Guide) and P11D(b) before completing this form.

## A Cars and car fuel

**1. Cars made available for private use**

If more than one car made available during the year, give details of each car at (a) and (b)

Make and model (a) ______________ ______ cc (b) ______________ ______ cc

| | | (a) '√' | (b) '√' |
|---|---|---|---|
| Value when new | £19,250 or less | ☐ | ☐ |
| | £19,251 - £29,000 | ☐ | ☐ |
| | more than £29,000 | ☐ | ☐ |
| First registered on or after 6.4.90 | | ☐ | ☐ |
| | before 6.4.90 | ☐ | ☐ |

Made available to director/employee from ______ to ______ from ______ to ______

Please indicate the annual business mileage travelled: '√'

- 2500 or less ☐
- 2501 - 17,999 ☐
- 18,000 or more ☐

The amount of any wages paid to a driver provided for the director/employee in respect of private journeys £ ______

Payment received from the director/employee for the private use of the car £ ______

You may wish to show the scale charges that you calculate apply to the car(s) provided using these boxes. Enter the taxable benefit (a) £ [ ] (b) £ [ ]

Will you please show here the price of a car or cars which are available in the tax year 1994-95 if you have not already given the Tax Office this information. Enter the price of the car and accessories. (a) £ [ ] (b) £ [ ]

**2. Car fuel "scale charges" - cars available for private use**

| | (a) Yes | (a) No | (b) Yes | (b) No |
|---|---|---|---|---|
| Was fuel for the car(s) provided other than for business travel? | ☐ | ☐ | ☐ | ☐ |
| If 'yes' was the director/employee required to make good the cost of all fuel used for private motoring including travel between home and normal place of work? | ☐ | ☐ | ☐ | ☐ |
| If the director/employee was required to make good the cost did he/she actually do so? | ☐ | ☐ | ☐ | ☐ |

If 'No' or if the director/employee was not required to make good the cost of fuel used for private motoring please indicate the type of engine (a) ☐ Petrol ☐ Diesel (b) ☐ Petrol ☐ Diesel

You may wish to show the scale charges that you calculate apply to the car fuel provided using these boxes. Enter the taxable benefit (a) £ [ ] (b) £ [ ]

**3. Car owned or hired by director/employee**

Allowances paid to the director/employee in respect of the use of the car and/or running and overhead expenses £ ______

Sum contributed by you towards the purchase price, depreciation or hire of a car £ ______

For official use

**P11D(1993)**

## B Beneficial loans

4 Enter details of loans made to, or arranged for, a director/employee (or any of his or her relatives) on which no interest was paid or on which the amount of interest paid was less than interest at the official rate (see P11D (Guide)). Include Miras loans under £30,000 and loans to directors from overdrawn or current accounts with the company. Complete a separate column for each loan. **Note:** If the only loan(s) provided is within (c) below (eg season ticket loan) and the benefit does not exceed £300 there is no need to complete this section.

Where you know the purpose of the loan please tick the box applicable. Otherwise tick the 'Don't know' box.

| | '√' | '√' |
|---|---|---|
| (a) loan for purchase or improvement of a main residence on which interest is eligible for relief (see Booklet 480 Appendix 5) | ☐ | ☐ |
| (b) loan for a purpose eligible for interest relief, other than loans covered by (a) (see Booklet 480 Appendix 5) | ☐ | ☐ |
| (c) loan not eligible for interest relief | ☐ | ☐ |
| (d) loan given as part of a relocation package | ☐ | ☐ |
| Don't know | ☐ | ☐ |

You need not provide any further details for a loan within (b) above. For each loan not within (b) please enter:

| | | |
|---|---|---|
| • amount outstanding at 5.4.93 or date loan was made (if later) | £ ______ | £ ______ |
| • amount outstanding at 5.4.94 or date loan was discharged (if earlier) | £ ______ | £ ______ |
| • maximum amount outstanding at any time in the year | £ ______ | £ ______ |
| • total amount of interest paid by the borrower in the year to 5.4.94 (enter nil if none was paid) | £ ______ | £ ______ |
| • date loan was made or discharged in year to 5.4.94 (where applicable) | ______ | ______ |
| If any loans made by you were waived or written off in the year to 5.4.94 what was the amount waived or written off? | | £ ______ |

## C Relocation expenses payments and benefits qualifying for relief

| | TOTAL AMOUNT OVER £8,000 |
|---|---|
| 5 Enter the excess over £8,000 of the total amount of all qualifying expenses payments (the gross amount) [illegible] and qualifying living accommodation provided | |
| *Non qualifying relocation expenses should be returned at item 20 of Section D and not here.* | £ |

## D Other expenses payments and benefits etc

| | | Gross Amount £ | Amount made good by director/employee or amount from which tax has been deducted under PAYE £ |
|---|---|---|---|
| 6. | Private medical dental etc attention and treatment or insurance against the cost of such treatment | | |
| 7. | General expenses allowance | | |
| 8. | Travelling and subsistence | | |
| 9. | Vans made available for private use | | |
| 10. | Entertainment | | |
| 11. | Home telephone expenses paid or reimbursed { Rental | | |
| | { Calls | | |
| 12. | Mobile telephone. Tick box if available for private calls '√' ☐ Indicate number of appliances ☐ | | |
| 13. | Subscriptions | | |
| 14. | Goods or services supplied free or below market value | | |
| 15. | Vouchers and credit cards not returned elsewhere | | |
| 16. | Cars, property, furniture and other assets given or transferred to the director/employee | | |
| 17. | Nursery places provided for children of the director/employee | | |
| 18. | Educational assistance provided for the director/employee or members of his or her family | | |
| 19. | House, flat or other living accommodation provided for the director/employee *Please show address* ______ Cost £ ______ | | |
| 20. | Relocation expenses and payments not qualifying for relief under the Finance Act 1993 | | |
| 21. | Income tax paid to the Collector in the year to 5 April 1993 which a company failed to deduct from a director's remuneration | | |
| 22. | Other expenses and benefits eg National Insurance contributions, holidays, private legal, accountancy etc expenses, contributions towards house purchase and other household expenses such as wages and keep of personal or domestic staff and gardening expenses. This is not an exhaustive list. Please consider whether you provide any expenses payments or benefits which are not mentioned here. *Please give details* ______ | | |
| | | | |
| | | | |
| | **Totals** | | |

# Appendix VII
# FEU 50 payer's guide

## Introduction

The 1986 Finance Act introduced a withholding tax on payments made for a UK appearance of a non-resident entertainer or sportsman.

You, the payer, must take tax off these payments.

This booklet, which is only a guide and does not have any legal force, tells you about:

- how the system works;
- what you must do as a payer;
- the administration of the new scheme, and;
- the standard of service you can expect and the steps you can take if you are dissatisfied with the service provided.

You will find the law covering withholding tax in TA 1988 ss 555–558 and Income Tax Regulations 1987. You can buy a copy of these from HMSO bookshops and other booksellers.

To avoid repetition the term 'entertainer' is used in this booklet to cover both non-resident entertainers and sportsmen. Examples in the booklet assume a basic rate of tax of 25%.

If this guide does not answer your questions and you need any help please get in touch with:

Foreign Entertainers Unit
5th Floor
City House
140 Edmund Street
Birmingham, B3 2JH

Tel No 021 200 2616; Fax 021 233 3483

The Unit was set up to administer the legislation and is part of the Special Compliance Office. Further information on service and complaint's can be found in Section D on p 138 below.

# Section A

### *A1 How the scheme works*

Any payer who makes a payment to any person, which in any way arises directly or indirectly from a UK appearance by a non-resident entertainer must deduct tax at the basic rate.

There are certain exceptions from the scheme. You will find details in A8.

### *A2 What are payments?*

Payments include money (cash, cheques etc) and also a loan of money. The list below gives some examples of payments:

- appearance fees;
- achievement bonus;
- exhibition income;
- box office percentage;
- TV rights;
- broadcasting/media fees;
- tour income;
- tournament winnings;
- prize money;
- advertising income;
- merchandising income;
- endorsement fees;
- film fees.

The scheme also applies to transfers of assets, for example, an airline ticket provided for an entertainer. Where assets are transferred withholding does not apply to the payment for the acquisition of the asset. But tax should be accounted for on the transfer to the entertainer. See B2.

### *A3 Does it matter who gets the payments?*

The short answer is no!

Payments are within the system no matter who gets them. It does not need to be the entertainer who gets the payment. Any payment to an individual, partnership or company or trust, whether or not they are resident in the UK should have basic rate withheld.

### *A4 What type of appearance is covered?*

Any appearance by the entertainer in the UK in his or her character as an entertainer will be within the scheme. The only exception will be where he or she visits the UK as a private individual, for example, on holiday.

To take a simple case, the entertainer appears in his or her recognised profession. This might be an actor performing in the theatre or a golfer competing in the Open Championship.

But the scheme is much wider than this. It also covers promotional activities, advertising and endorsement of goods or services. This may include a photocall, TV or radio interview or other appearances.

The appearance does not have to be in front of an immediate audience. It includes work on film, video, radio and live or recorded television.

*A5 What is the link between the payment and the UK appearance?*

Any payment which arises directly or indirectly from a UK appearance will be within the scheme. In most cases it will be easy to find the link. For example, a tennis player wins Wimbledon prize money or a pop star is paid for appearing at a concert in Wembley.

The payment does not have to have a direct connection with the UK appearance. Endorsement fees paid to a tennis player using sports equipment in a UK tournament would be linked.

*A6 Which entertainers and sportsmen are involved?*

This list includes some examples – it is not exhaustive. Athletes, golfers, cricketers, footballers, tennis players, boxers, snooker players, darts players, motor racing drivers, jockeys, ice skaters, contestants in chess tournaments, pop starts, musicians, conductors, dancers, actors, TV and radio personalities, variety artistes. The person may appear alone or with others in teams, choirs, bands, orchestras, opera companies, ballet companies, troupes, circuses.

*A7 How do I know whether they are non-resident in the UK?*

In most cases it will be obvious.

You may know from the agent or management company, perhaps from the need to get a work permit or clear immigration formalities.

A UK national who is not-resident comes within the scheme so it should not be assumed that withholding applies only to overseas nationals.

If there is any uncertainty about the entertainer's residence position you should get in touch with the Foreign Entertainers Unit. They will advise you.

*A8 Which payments are excepted from withholding tax?*

If you already deduct tax under the Taxes Acts you do not have to withhold further tax. This will apply, for example, where tax is deducted at source either on copyright royalties (TA 1988 s 536) or under PAYE.

You do not normally have to withhold tax on amounts paid for ancillary services to a person who is resident and ordinarily resident in the UK. This includes, for example, payments for:

- hall hire;
- security;
- damages/carpentry;
- stage hands;
- PA equipment;
- lighting etc;
- equipment hire;
- advertising;
- ticket printing;
- hire of chairs, barriers or marquee etc.

You do not have to withhold tax on payments to an entertainer for record sales (including black vinyl, pre-recorded music cassettes or compact disc) where the payment is based on the proceeds of sales or is a non-returnable advance on account of future sales.

Do not withhold tax if the total payments to an individual or group, including any connected payments by an associate etc, will be £1,000 or less during the tax year. (The tax year runs from 6 April in one year to 5 April in the following year.)

The total payment for this purpose includes not only cash but also expenses paid on behalf of the artiste such as air fares or the cost of any asset transferred to the artiste.

If you are making the first payment and it is less than £1,000 but you know in advance (for example, from the contract) that the total payments for the tax year will be more than £1,000 then you should deduct tax even from the first payment.

If you do not know the total amount of payments for the year then you should deduct tax from each payment.

*Example*

The payer knows in advance that he will be making total payments of £1,200, made in three instalments.

| | | £ |
|---|---|---|
| 1st payment | = | 400 |
| *Less* tax withheld at 25% | = | 100 |
| Net payment to entertainer | = | 300 |
| 2nd payment | = | 400 |
| *Less* tax withheld at 25% | = | 100 |
| Net payment to entertainer | = | 300 |
| 3rd payment | = | 400 |
| *Less* tax withheld at 25% | = | 100 |
| Net payment to entertainer | = | 300 |
| Total payments | = | 1,200 |
| Tax withheld | = | 300 |
| Net payments | = | 900 |

There are no other exceptions to the scheme.

Even if the payments you withhold tax from may not ultimately be assessed on the recipient (for example, because they are protected by a Double Taxation Agreement) you must not exclude these payments from the scheme.

If you are in any doubt at all about which payments are excluded from the scheme please ask the Foreign Entertainers Unit for advice.

## Section B

### *B1 What the payer has to do*

Each time you make a payment you must deduct tax at basic rate unless an arrangement has been made with the Foreign Entertainers Unit (see B6 to B9). The Inland Revenue does not need to make an assessment.

If you do not deduct tax you will be held responsible for the tax due.

### *B2 How to work out the tax*

Where you are paying money it is very straightforward to work out the tax.

Assuming the basic rate percentage for the year of payment is 25% deduct this percentage from each payment made.

#### *Example*

| | | £ |
|---|---|---|
| Gross payment | = | 5,000 |
| Tax (£5,000 × 25%) | = | 1,250 |
| Net amount paid to entertainer | | 3,750 |

The same applies to a loan of money. You should deduct tax from the amount you lend.

Payments to the Inland Revenue of tax withheld should be made in sterling. If you make a payment directly or indirectly to an entertainer in a foreign currency you should calculate the withholding tax due using the rate of exchange at the time when the payment is made. The rate of exchange adopted should be shown on your return form FEU 1.

If the transfer of an asset is involved (for example, a motor car for a 'hole in one' during a golf competition) you must account for the tax as if the asset's cost to you or in connection with providing it was the net amount of the payment.

#### *Example*

The car costs you £3,750. You need to work out the gross amount of the payment and deduct tax on that amount. To work out the gross amount you do the following sum.

$$\text{Net amount of payment} \times \frac{25 \text{ (basic rate of tax)}}{75 \text{ (100 less basic rate of tax)}}$$

£3,750 × $^{25}/_{75}$ = £1,250

Add the result to the net payment to get the gross payment.

£1,250 + £3,750 = £5,000

Tax (£5,000 × 25%) = £1,250

If the payment you make is made out of a payment you have received for the same UK appearance (that is, it is one of a series of payments) then you may 'frank' (treat as paid) your payment to the extent that it has already suffered tax.

*Example*

*Withholding tax*

A engages, via a management company B Ltd, a non-resident entertainer, C, to appear in his theatre in the UK.
B Ltd is resident in the UK and C is the only non-resident entertainer it engages in the quarter. The sequence of payments is:

A pays £100,000 less £25,000 tax to B Ltd
B Ltd pays £60,000 less £15,000 tax to C
B Ltd is liable to account to the Inland Revenue for £15,000 but as the payment he has received has had £25,000 withholding tax deducted from it he can treat the £15,000 as paid.

*Entries on B Ltd's return form FEU 1*

The amount and income tax columns of B's return for the relevant period should be completed as follows:

| | *Amount* | *Tax* |
|---|---|---|
| | £60,000 | £15,000 |
| Less already paid | | £15,000 |
| Tax payable now | | Nil |

Evidence of the tax already suffered should be provided with the return using form FEU 2 supplied by A.

You will find details of how the payment is treated in B Ltd's company accounts and of the repayment of tax in certain circumstances at B10.

### *B3 How do you account for the tax?*

You must account for tax withheld within 14 days after the end of the return period during which the payment was made. The return periods for each tax year are:

- 30 June
- 30 September

- 31 December
- 5 April.

*B4 Filling in form FEU 1*

Complete form FEU 1 as soon as possible after the end of the relevant period and in any case within 14 days of the end of the period. The form itself gives you instructions on completion.

Then send the completed form FEU 1 and the total withholding tax payable to the Accounts Office Shipley within 14 days of the relevant period.

If the return of tax is late you may become liable to interest and/or penalties.

Please note that the return form FEU 1 is due from the payer without the Inland Revenue notifying you. It is now your responsibility to make a Return.

New payers should contact Foreign Entertainers Unit who will issue the appropriate Starter Pack.

The Accounts Office Shipley will send you replacement forms FEU 1 before the end of each Return period. If you want to use your own design of form FEU 1 you must submit it to the Foreign Entertainers Unit for approval before you do so.

*B5 What record does the payee get of the payment?*

Whenever you make a payment you must complete a form FEU 2.

This form is in 3 parts:

- Part 1 Send to Accounts Office Shipley along with your form FEU 1 Return.
- Part 2 Keep this for your own records.
- Part 3 Send this to the payee as a certificate of the payment made and tax withheld.

On no account should you issue a duplicate form FEU 2. If the payee loses the original certificate tell him or her to contact the Foreign Entertainers Unit.

If you are not deducting withholding tax because the payment is under the £1,000 threshold (see A8) or no tax is deducted because of an arrangement with the Inland Revenue (see B7 to B9) you do not need to complete a form FEU 2.

*B6 Arrangements with the Revenue to limit the amount of tax withheld*

An arrangement may be made in writing between the Foreign Entertainers Unit, the payer and the entertainer or other recipient. This arrangement allows the payer to deduct an amount which is less than the basic rate of tax. The purpose of such an arrangement is to deduct an amount which corresponds as closely as possible to the entertainer's final liability on the payment.

Any applications that a payment should be subject to a reduced tax payment must be made in writing. Any letter which advises the Unit that detailed figures are to follow is considered to constitute an advance notification of an application but does not constitute the application itself.

The time for making an application is not later than 30 days before the payment is due to be made.

The payer and the entertainer or other recipient can make an application either singly or jointly. If the application is not accepted tax must be withheld at the basic rate on all payments.

## *B7 Applying for an arrangement*

You and/or the entertainer will have to give the information needed for the Inspector to make a decision on whether or not to grant an arrangement. This includes:

- dates of arrival in and departure from the UK;
- whether the entertainer is likely to return to the UK again before the next 5 April;
- a projection of income with details of dates and venues;
- an itemised projection of the expenses which will be incurred;
- a copy of any contract covering appearances.

The application should have sufficient information to show how figures have been arrived at (including the basis for any estimates) and how expenditure common to several countries has been apportioned.

The Inspector will also take into account whether you are making a payment on account of the withholding tax due or whether a guarantee has been given.

In some cases, you may be authorised not to deduct any tax from a payment. This would apply, for example, if a pop star prior to a UK tour undertook to pay in advance (or secured by bank guarantee) all the UK tax expected from the tour.

In other cases, you may be authorised to deduct either a reduced rate of tax or a fixed sum from the gross payment. This could apply, for example, where an entertainer has to meet substantial expenditure out of a gross fee thus reducing the expected UK tax liability.

In reaching an agreement the Inspector will make allowances for admissible expenses. What can be allowed depends on the general rules covering expenditure allowable under Case I and II of Schedule D and on the facts of each case. Normally allowances will be made for:

- general subsistence expenses;
- commission, manager's and agent's fees;
- UK travelling;
- international air fares to and from the UK where an artiste comes to the UK for an activity and returns directly to his or her home country.

Other expenses may be allowable. What is allowable in each case will need to be agreed with Foreign Entertainers Unit including the proportion of any costs common to several countries.

### *B8 How do you know that a reduced tax payment has been authorised?*

The Foreign Entertainers Unit will authorise you to deduct a reduced amount of tax by sending you a form FEU 4. Even where you have been a party to the agreed arrangement with the Inland Revenue you must wait until you get the form FEU 4.

If you have not received a certificate on form FEU 4 when you come to make the payment you must deduct tax at the basic rate from the gross payment you make.

### *B9 Action*

If you are making a reduced tax payment you must return the details and account for the tax withheld by filing in the return form FEU 1. B3 to B4 tells you about the form FEU 1.

### *B10 How are payments dealt with in your Schedule D or corporation tax accounts?*

If income you receive is attributed to the entertainer under the rules set out in TA 1988 s 556 and Income Tax Regulations 1987 reg 7 then the tax withheld from the payment you receive will be treated as a payment on account of the entertainer's UK liability.

You will not be charged to UK tax on that income and there will be no repayment of the withholding tax to you.

But if

- you are UK resident; and
- the income you receive is not attributed to the entertainer under the rules above the payment you receive will be a receipt of your business.

The amount of the assessable income will be the payment received plus the amount of the withholding tax which has been deducted. You will be able to claim the gross payment you make as a deduction in your UK income tax or corporation tax accounts.

'Gross payment' means the payment to the entertainer or intermediary plus the tax accounted for to the Inland Revenue.

If you make the payment in a series of payments as described at B2, that is, a franked payment, you may be entitled to set off tax withheld from payments you receive against your UK tax liabilities or claim a repayment of tax.

*Example*

A, a UK resident, pays B Ltd, also a UK resident, £100,000 for C's services. C is a non-resident entertainer. C is paid a £60,000 fee by B Ltd.

*Withholding tax*

| | £ | |
|---|---|---|
| A pays | 100,000 | |
| Less tax at 25% | 25,000 | paid to Inland Revenue |
| | 75,000 | net to B Ltd |
| B Ltd pays | 60,000 | |
| Less tax at 25% | 15,000 | (this sum is franked out of the £25,000 already deducted) |
| | 45,000 | paid to C |

*Treatment in the accounts*

A is allowed an expense of £100,000 (that is the gross payment shown in his accounts).
B Ltd credits a receipt of £100,000 as income and is allowed an expense of £60,000 in its accounts.

*Tax set offs*

B Ltd can set the excess withholding tax of £10,000 (that is £25,000 less the franked payment of £15,000) against its income tax/corporation tax liability.
If B Ltd had a tax liability of less than £10,000 it can claim a repayment of the amount by which £10,000 exceeds its income tax/corporation tax liability.

### *B11 How do you cope with payment chains?*

Some activities may give rise to a chain of payments. For example, money for a concert may flow from a venue to a promoter then to the artiste. Every payer in the chain must deduct tax as required by law.

If a payer higher up the chain has already deducted tax then you must take this into account in deciding how much tax, if any, you need to deduct (see B2 and B10).

Payers can ask for an arrangement (see B6) which moves the withholding point further down the chain so that payments between specified payers can be made witbout deduction of tax. This can only be done with the Foreign Entertainers Unit's approval.

*Example*

A concert is arranged at a hall. The venue owners control the box office and pay over the ticket proceeds less a percentage deduction to the concert promoter. He deducts his costs before paying an agreed amount to the artiste.

If the concert promoter makes a 'middleman' application the Unit may agree to nil withholding on the venue payments leaving the promoter as the withholding point. The promoter will then have to deduct tax at basic rate on his or her payment or a reduced amount if an artiste's application has been made and agreed in a lower sum.

The Unit will ask for certain information in support of any 'middleman' application you make, for example, a copy of any contract, dates of appearances, and probably a copy of the budget. If you are submitting a 'middleman' application for the first time the Unit will be happy to advise you on the procedure and level of information required.

## Section C

### *C1 Assessments*

Withholding tax will be due and payable without the making of an assessment. Any tax paid late may be liable to an interest charge.

If a payer does not deduct withholding tax from a payment or does not pay over tax which he/she has deducted, the Inland Revenue may make an assessment to recover the tax due direct from the payer.

An assessment may be made on the payments made in the tax year or for a particular period (see B3). The tax charged in the assessment will be due and payable on or before whichever is the earlier of the normal due date (see B3) or the 14th day after the date of the notice of assessment.

You will see therefore that there is no advantage in delaying payment and waiting for an assessment. The tax will be treated as due at the normal time and interest calculated accordingly.

### *C2 Appeals*

Any appeal against an assessment made to recover withholding tax should be made in writing to the Foreign Entertainers Unit. The appeal should be made within 30 days from the date the notice of assessment was issued. Please use form 64-7 (New) to make your appeal.

### *C3 Interest*

Interest may be charged and recovered by the Inland Revenue in any of the following circumstances:

- withholding tax paid late. This will apply whether paid late without an assessment or recovered by assessment;
- return form FEU 1 submitted late;
- an incorrect return having been made.

### *C4 Penalties*

Penalties may be due where the payer fails to make a return on form FEU 1 or submits an incorrect Return on form FEU 1.

### *C5 Information and inspection*

The Foreign Entertainers Unit inspector will be able, provided due notice is given, to call for information from payers. The information which the Inspector can request is fully set out in the Income Tax (Entertainers and Sportsmen) Regulations 1987 reg 9.

## Section D

### *D1 Where can I get help and information?*

Any questions which are not answered in this guide may be referred to the Foreign Entertainers Unit. The address, telephone number and fax number of the Unit can be found in the introduction to this booklet. The Unit's staff will try and help you with any practical problems you have in complying with the scheme.

Your professional adviser may also wish to help you deal with practical points arising from the law.

### *D2 What service can I expect?*

'You can expect to be treated fairly and efficiently by the Foreign Entertainers Unit which will handle each case in accord with the Taxpayer's Charter. This states:

> 'You are entitled to expect the Inland Revenue
>
> To be fair
> - by settling your tax affairs impartially
> - by expecting you to pay only what is due under the law
> - by treating everyone with equal fairness
>
> To help you
> - to get your tax affairs right
> - to understand your rights and obligations
> - by providing clear leaflets and forms
> - by giving you information and assistance at our enquiry offices
> - by being courteous at all times
>
> To provide an efficient service
> - by settling your tax affairs promptly and accurately
> - by keeping your private affairs strictly confidential
> - by using the information you give us only as allowed by law
> - by keeping to a minimum your costs of complying with the law
> - by keeping our costs down
>
> To be accountable for what we do
> - by setting standards for ourselves and publishing how well we live up to them

If you are not satisfied
- we will tell you exactly how to complain
- you can ask for your tax affairs to be looked at again
- you can appeal to an independent tribunal
- your MP can refer your complaint to the Ombudsman

In return we need you
- to be honest
- to give us accurate information
- to pay your tax on time'

## *D3 What can I do if I am not happy with the service I receive?*

Naturally we hope that this question will not arise.

If you have a complaint, first write to the Head of the Foreign Entertainers Unit. His or her name is to be found on correspondence from the Unit or can be obtained by telephoning 021 200 2616. He or she will do everything possible to resolve the problem quickly. Most complaints are settled satisfactorily at this level.

If after this you are still unhappy you can take the matter further by writing to the

Customer Service Manager
Inland Revenue
Special Compliance Office
Angel Court
199 Borough High Street
London
SE1 1HZ

If the Customer Service Manager is unable to settle a complaint to your satisfaction, there are still two options open to you. The first is to write to the Inland Revenue's Head Office at:

Somerset House
Strand
London
WC2R 1LB

The second is to ask your MP to take up your case with the Inland Revenue or with the Treasury Ministers.

If you feel that the Inland Revenue has not handled your tax affairs properly, your MP may ask the Independent Parliamentary Commissioner for Administration, commonly known as the Ombudsman, to review your case.

## *D4 How else can I help?*

Another way you can help is by telling us what you think of the service we offer. We would value your opinion – for example, on the way we dealt with your tax affairs.

You may even have particular ideas for improving our service. If you do, please let us know by writing to the Customer Service Manager quoting your FEU reference number which can be found on all correspondence sent to you.

## List of forms

The forms shown below are those that the payer will be involved with:

| | |
|---|---|
| FEU 1 | Return of payments made to non-resident entertainers |
| FEU 1 (CS) | Payer's return continuation sheet |
| FEU 1 (Reminder) | Payer's return reminder |
| FEU 2 | Foreign Entertainers Unit tax deduction certificate |
| FEU 4 | Payer's notification that basic rate withholding tax is not appropriate |
| FEU 40 | Stationery request |
| FEU 50 | Payer's guide |

The forms shown below are those that the payee will be involved with

| | |
|---|---|
| FEU 2 | Foreign Entertainers Unit tax deduction certificate |
| FEU 5 | Payee's repayment claim form |
| FEU 7 | Provisional liabilities |
| FEU 8 | Application for reduced tax payment |
| FEU 12 | Payee's return |

# Appendix VIII
# Local taxation of income earned overseas

The purpose of this appendix is to outline the overseas tax position of a UK resident performer performing in the following countries:

- United States;
- Australia;
- France;
- Germany;
- The Netherlands;
- Republic of Ireland;
- Japan.

It does not address other aspects of performing in, or deriving income from, the above countries, such as immigration and exchange control requirements. Additionally, the appendix only addresses the position where UK performers or companies are taxable in the relevant country and does not examine the potential advantages of organising the activities through a third country to derive the benefits of other double tax treaties. Care must be taken if 'treaty shopping' as increasingly double taxation treaties are being amended to prevent their use in this way.

## The use of tax treaties

The starting point when looking at the overseas tax position is to determine the performer's position under the overseas country's domestic tax legislation. This is not the end of the matter, however, since relief may be available under the relevant comprehensive double tax treaty which the UK may have negotiated with the overseas country.

These treaties contain detailed provisions to eliminate double taxation on income and capital gains. Their objective is to ensure that, if a person is resident in one country but receives income from another, the income is not taxed in both countries or, if it is, the total tax imposed by the two countries is reduced to the higher of the two taxes.

Residence for treaty purposes is defined in each treaty. Most modern treaties contain provisions to prevent individuals being dually resident. Thus an individual resident outside the UK who receives UK source income may benefit from:

(1) exemption, or tax charged at a reduced rate, eg on interest and royalties;

(2) credit, ie where income remains doubly taxed, one country's tax is credited against tax charged in the other country on the same income.

Similarly, an individual working abroad and receiving foreign source income, but remaining UK resident, may also benefit although in most countries such relief is denied to artistes and athletes.

Many double tax treaties allow residents of a tax treaty country to claim partial personal allowances in the same way as a British subject resident abroad.

In the absence of a tax treaty, credit is given against the UK tax liability of UK residents for foreign income taxes paid on doubly taxed overseas income. Non-residents may be able to claim a corresponding relief, but must look to foreign tax legislation.

## OECD Model Treaty

It is not practicable to examine the lengthy and complex provisions of every country. It is, however, useful to examine the terms of the OECD Model Double Taxation Convention (the latest text is of the third version dated 1992) which forms the basis of many of the treaties which the UK has negotiated.

Articles 7, 14 and 15 of the Model Treaty broadly provide that an individual who is a resident of one contracting state should be exempt from tax in the other contracting state where he works there for short periods and his work is not connected with a 'permanent establishment' in that state.

### Article 17

Article 17 of the model convention, covering artistes and athletes, states:

> '(1) Notwithstanding the provisions of Articles 14 and 15, income derived by a resident of a Contracting State as an entertainer, such as a theatre, motion picture, radio or television artiste, or a musician, or as a sportsman, from his personal activities as such exercised in the other Contracting State, may be taxed in that other State.
>
> (2) Where income in respect of personal activities exercised by an entertainer or a sportsman in his capacity as such accrues not to the entertainer or sportsman himself but to another person, that income may, notwithstanding the provisions of Articles 7, 14 and 15, be taxed in the Contracting State in which the activities of the entertainer or sportsman are exercised.'

The effect of Article 17 is to allow a contracting state to tax entertainers and sportsmen in respect of income derived from activities in that State. Paragraph 2 permits the contracting state to tax the income even if it is not received directly by the entertainer or sportsman himself but by some other party, possibly with no permanent establishment in that state, eg where an entertainer is employed by a 'loan-out' or 'artiste' company.

The use of an Article such as this has become extremely commonplace as can be seen from Appendix IX.

## Article 12

Article 12 of the model convention deals with royalties and again is typical of such articles in many modern treaties which the UK has negotiated. Its provisions are as follows:

> '(1) Royalties arising in a Contracting State and paid to a resident of the other Contracting State shall be taxable only in the other State if such resident is the beneficial owner of the royalties.
>
> (2) The term "royalties" as used in this Article means payments of any kind received as a consideration for the use of, or the right to use, any copyright of literary, artistic or scientific work including cinematographic films, any patent, trademark, design or model, plan, secret formula or process, or for information concerning industrial, commercial or scientific experience.
>
> (3) The provisions of paragraph 1 shall not apply if the beneficial owner of the royalties, being a resident of a Contracting State, carries on business in the other Contracting State in which the royalties arise, through a permanent establishment situated therein, or performs in that other State independent personal services from a fixed base situated therein, and the right or property in respect of which the royalties are paid is effectively connected with such permanent establishment or fixed base. In such case the provisions of Article 7 or Article 14, as the case may be, shall apply.
>
> (4) Where, by reason of a special relationship between the payer and the beneficial owner or between both of them and some other person, the amount of the royalties, having regard to the use, right or information for which they are paid, exceeds the amount which would have been agreed upon by the payer and the beneficial owner in the absence of such relationship, the provisions of this Article shall apply only to the last-mentioned amount. In such case, the excess part of the payments shall remain taxable according to the laws of each Contracting State, due regard being had to the other provisions of this Convention.'

Although the model treaty exempts royalties from taxation in the State in which they arise, a number of countries reserve the right to apply tax, and details of these withholdings are included in Appendix IX.

It will be noted from the above that a distinction is drawn between income derived from activities actually carried out in a state and income, eg royalties, derived from that state. It is important when structuring arrangements to try to avoid aggregating sources of income such that they become associated with activities carried on in the contracting state. For example, where sponsorship arrangements are entered into, the payment may cover many different things, eg venue advertising, support for costs incurred, use of the performer's name, recorded interviews etc. A careful review of the component parts may allow separate arrangements to be structured, some of which will be taxed as connected with the activities but hopefully some will be separable and therefore the foreign tax can be avoided either totally or perhaps levied at the, normally lower, royalty withholding rate.

# United States

## Domestic law

It is possible for a non-US citizen normally resident outside the US to be considered a resident alien for US tax purposes. If this is the case he will be taxed, in the absence of any treaty relief, on his worldwide income in the same manner as a US citizen. An individual can be regarded as a resident alien in any calendar year if he meets either of two tests:

(1) if he has permanent immigrant status under US immigration law, ie a green card holder; or
(2) if he has substantial presence, as defined, in the US in a calendar year.

An individual is regarded as having a substantial presence in the US if he is there for at least 31 days during the calendar year and if the days in the current year plus $\frac{1}{3}$ of the days in the preceding year plus $\frac{1}{6}$ of the days in the second preceding year are equal to or in excess of 183 days. An individual is treated as present in the US on a day if he is physically present in the US at any time during that day.

The substantial presence test will not be applied where an individual is in the US for less than 183 days in a year and has a tax home in a foreign country and a closer connection with that foreign country, unless the individual has taken steps to apply for permanent resident status.

A non-resident alien who is not treaty protected is currently taxed:

(1) at graduated rates on all income from US sources which is effectively connected with the conduct of a trade or business, including employment, in the US (in some cases, income from non-US sources may also be taxable);
(2) at a flat 30% on fixed or determinable periodical income from US sources such as royalties.

The only relief for non-resident aliens provided by US domestic legislation allows a foreign individual to receive remuneration for personal services performed in the US free of tax provided:

(1) he does not spend more than 90 days in the US in the calendar year;
(2) his total income for those services is US$3,000 or less; and
(3) he performs the services as an employee of, or under a contract with, an alien not resident in the US, a foreign partnership or a foreign corporation not engaged in US trade or business.

To prevent a foreign taxpayer from avoiding or mitigating US tax by receiving income in a year after his US trade or business has ceased the Tax Reform Act of 1986 provides that, effective from 1 January 1987, the income of a non-resident alien for a tax year attributable to a transaction in another tax year will be treated as effectively connected with the conduct of a US trade or business if it would have been so treated if it were taken into account on the other tax year.

**Treaty relief**

In the case of the UK, the double tax treaty between the two countries serves to modify the position outlined in the previous paragraphs. The general position under the treaty is as follows:

*Royalties*

Royalties beneficially owned by a UK resident and derived from the US are exempt from tax in the US under Article 12. This exemption only applies where the person receiving the royalties is a resident of the UK and beneficially owns the royalty. It does not, therefore, apply where an intermediary, such as an agent or nominee, who is a resident of the UK, collects or receives the royalties on behalf of a non-resident.

Royalties within the meaning of the Article, are payments of any kind received as consideration for the use of, or the right to use, any copyright of literary or artistic work, but not including cinematographic films or films or tapes used for radio or television broadcasting. Payments within the exclusion are dealt with as business profits and are therefore taxable at graduated rates if they are connected with a permanent establishment in the US. The same treatment applies to royalties generally if they are connected with a fixed base which the entertainer has in the US.

It is important to note that in this regard, for the UK resident to benefit from the treaty, he must demonstrate that the receipts are true royalties. In order to do this, he must have or have passed to the payer a property interest in the relevant copyright. A mere payment for personal services, where the payer has always held the relevant copyright, calculated on the basis of sales does not constitute a royalty for these purposes even though the payment may be calculated on the basis of sales and described as a 'royalty' in the agreement.

It is understood that the US Internal Revenue Service (IRS) has advanced arguments that private houses, extended tours and recording studios used in the US constitute fixed bases for the purposes of the treaty. The commentary in the OECD model treaty and an IRS ruling suggest that the existence of a stage for a concert will not constitute a permanent establishment. It is the opinion of the US Treasury that a 'fixed base' and a 'permanent establishment' are one and the same thing.

*Income from independent personal services (self-employed)*

The general position under the treaty is that a UK resident individual is taxable in the US if either:

(1) he spends more than 183 days in the US in the calendar year; or
(2) he has a fixed base regularly available to him in the US.

*Income from dependent personal services (employees)*

The general position under the treaty is that a UK resident individual is taxable in the US in respect of services performed there unless:

(1) he is present in the US for less than 183 days in the calendar year;
(2) the remuneration is paid by, or on behalf of, an employer who is not a resident of the US; and
(3) the remuneration is not borne by a permanent establishment or fixed base which the employer has in the US.

## Taxation of artistes and athletes: Article 17

This Article deals with the taxability of artistes and athletes, and removes from them the treaty benefits which, in the absence of the Article, might accrue to them in respect of their income earned as artistes or athletes, as set out above.

The main effect of the provision is to curtail the use of 'loan-out' companies which were designed to ensure that entertainers employed by companies not resident in the US in respect of services rendered in the US were exempt from US tax under the predecessor of Article 15 if they spent less than 183 days there. A combination of this exemption and the availability of 365-day relief in the UK as described on p 81 to 84 meant that a UK resident entertainer could avoid paying any tax on such income.

Prior to the introduction of the 1975 US/UK treaty, the IRS had attacked such loan-out arrangements by the issue of Revenue Rulings 73–330 and 73–331 (the 'Lend a Star' Rulings) under which the IRS took the position that, unless certain criteria were met, the entertainer would be considered an independent contractor and tax would have to be withheld when payments were made.

In view of the importance of the US as a market, it is well worth examining this Article in detail.

### *Taxation of the individual artiste or athlete*

Article 17(1) provides as follows:

> 'Notwithstanding the provisions of Article 14 (Independent personal services) and 15 (Dependent personal services), income derived by entertainers, such as theatre, motion picture, radio or television artistes, and musicians, and by athletes, from their personal activities as such may be taxed in the Contracting State in which these activities are exercised, except where the amount of the gross receipts derived by an entertainer or athlete, including expenses reimbursed to him or borne on his behalf, from such activities do not exceed 15,000 United States dollars or its equivalent in pounds sterling in the tax year concerned.'

Under the domestic laws of each country, artistes and athletes will be taxed in their country of residence and, in the case of US citizens, in the US whatever the country of their residence. However, this paragraph provides that a resident of the UK may be taxed in the US in respect of the income generated from activities exercised in the United States except where the gross receipts derived do not exceed US$15,000 in any calendar year.

This paragraph overrides Article 14 (Independent personal services) and Article 15 (Dependent personal services). Accordingly, neither artistes nor athletes undertaking activities in the US, either on their own account or as employees of another person, can benefit from the 183-day rule set out at p 146 above. They are taxable in the US if their gross receipts from activities undertaken there exceed US$15,000, however short their stay.

Gross receipts include not only performance fees and prize money, but also expenses reimbursed to the entertainer or athlete, or borne on his behalf. Expenses borne on behalf of the entertainer or athlete include any expenditure borne by a third party, wherever resident and wherever the money was paid, in respect of travel, meals and lodgings, payments to persons such as band members or agents, and any other amount which is generally related to the US activities of the artiste or athlete.

The US$15,000 limitation refers to total gross receipts in a tax year, not total gross receipts per engagement.

An artiste or athlete resident in the UK whose gross receipts in respect of activities undertaken in the US are US$14,999 in a tax year escapes taxation in the US. A similar artiste or athlete whose gross receipts are US$15,001 is taxed on the full amount of taxable income arising. Accordingly, the artiste or athlete whose gross receipts only amount to US$14,999 may well, in after-tax terms, be better off than a colleague whose gross receipts are US$2 more. This is subject to the impact of double tax credit relief or foreign tax credit as appropriate.

It should be noted that, where a resident of the US is working in the UK, the US$15,000 limitation is to be taken as its equivalent in pounds sterling in the tax year concerned. No guidance is given on how to determine the exchange rate to use, although the wording 'equivalent in pounds sterling in the tax year concerned' indicates that the average rate for the year might be used. However, as a practical matter, it may well be that the US$15,000 limitation is determined by reference to the rate of exchange in force when the activities are performed.

The treaty does not provide for the deductibility in computing taxable income of expenses incurred by the artiste or athlete. Accordingly, artistes and athletes will only be able to deduct those expenses allowed by the domestic legislation of the country in which they are undertaking their activities.

The limitation of US$15,000 was included in the first signed draft of the treaty in December 1975. There is no apparent intention to adjust the figure for inflation. Assuming only 8% annual inflation since the first draft of the treaty was signed in December 1975, the limitation, if it had been adjusted for inflation, should have been some US$22,000 on the date of ratification and by now would be some $60,000. In practice, it is felt that the exemption will not be of great significance to most performers, given the high level of their earnings although it may be of use to some sportsmen competing in events on a one-off basis.

It should be noted that certain persons in the cultural and arts world are not affected by this article, eg painters, authors, television directors, producers and scriptwriters.

### *Taxation of employer*

Article 17(2) reads as follows:

> 'Where income in respect of personal activities as such of an entertainer or athlete accrues not to that entertainer or athlete himself but to another person, that income may, notwithstanding the provisions of Articles 7 (Business profits), 14 (Independent personal services) and 15 (Dependent personal services), be taxed in the Contracting State in which the activities of the entertainer or athlete are exercised. For the purposes of the preceding sentence, income of an entertainer or athlete shall be deemed not to accrue to another person if it is established that neither the entertainer or athlete, nor persons related thereto, participate directly or indirectly in the profits of such other person in any manner, including the receipt of deferred remuneration, bonuses, fees, dividends, partnership distributions or other distributions.'

Paragraph 2 is concerned with cases where income accrues to a third party in respect of the activities of an entertainer or athlete. It thus covers the situation where a company is formed in order to exploit the abilities of an artiste or athlete, with the company receiving the performance fees and paying the artiste or athlete a salary.

Paragraph 2 states that, when income in respect of the personal activities of an artiste or athlete accrues to a person other than the artiste or athlete, that person can be taxed in the country where the activities were performed on the income arising from these activities. No protection can be claimed under Article 7 (Business profits), Article 14 (Independent personal services) or Article 15 (Dependent personal services).

The artiste or athlete himself will also be taxed in respect of his salary, or other fee received from the third party, if his gross receipts exceed US$15,000. No other person to whom income accrues is entitled to the US$15,000 exemption to which the individual artiste or athlete is entitled. Moreover, since the provisions of Article 7 (Business profits) are overridden, the right under that Article to deduct an allocation or a proportion of head office overheads and other centrally incurred expenses from the income accruing is lost, although the general right to such deductions under US law may remain.

The other person may be a corporation or company, trust, individual or partnership. The nature of the person will determine the kind of tax and, accordingly, the rates of tax, to be imposed on the income accruing.

The paragraph contains one very tightly drawn relieving provision. Income in respect of the services of an artiste or athlete shall not be deemed to accrue to another person if that person can establish, presumably to the satisfaction of the competent authority of the state in which the activities were carried on, that neither the artiste or athlete, nor persons related to him, will participate directly or indirectly in the profits of the other person. If this can be shown (eg in the case of a charity performance) then, if the other person is a resident of the UK, that person will not be taxable in the US on the income if the activities of the artiste or athlete were undertaken in the US unless that person is carrying on business there through a permanent establishment. In other words, the tax position is determined as if Article 17 did not exist.

As stated above, however, the provision is tightly drawn. The test is failed if the artiste or athlete participates directly or indirectly in the profits of the other person, and direct or indirect participation includes the receipt of deferred remuneration, bonuses, fees, dividends, partnership distributions or other distributions.

The test is also failed if any person related to the artiste or athlete participates directly or indirectly in the profits of the other person. The treaty does not comment on the definition of a person related to an artiste or athlete. However, it has been stated that a person may be considered to be related to the artiste or athlete if he is regularly employed by the artiste or athlete in an advisory capacity, such as his solicitor, accountant or investment adviser.

The definition of 'associated enterprise' in Article 9(5) (Associated enterprises) is stated by the US Treasury Technical Explanation to be irrelevant in this context.

It should be noted that, in view of the treaty provisions, US promoters etc are reluctant to pay over gross fees to entertainers and will usually insist on withholding 30% to be paid to the IRS. This can have a significant cashflow disadvantage, and it is advisable to obtain advance by submitting a budget of expected net income to the IRS and paying a tax deposit equivalent to the tax calculated on the budget profit.

### *Tax rates*

These are shown in Appendix XI.

# Australia

## Domestic law

A resident of Australia is taxable upon all income from all sources on a similar basis to that applying in the UK.

An individual who is not resident in Australia is subject to Australian tax on income from Australian sources. Royalties paid by Australian residents to non-residents are subject to withholding tax.

## Treaty relief

The double tax treaty between the UK and Australia modifies this basic position and the general position can be summarised as follows:

### *Royalties*

Article 10 of the treaty states that Australian tax on royalties derived and beneficially owned by a UK resident shall not exceed 10% of the gross amount of the royalties. The exemption does not apply where an intermediary, such as an agent or nominee, who is resident in the UK receives the royalty on behalf of somebody who is not so resident, nor where the UK resident has a permanent establishment in Australia with which the royalties are effectively connected.

The definition of 'royalty' for treaty purposes includes payments of any kind to the extent to which they are paid as consideration for the use of, or the right to use, copyright or motion picture films, films or video tapes for use in connection with television or tapes for use in connection with radio broadcasting.

Where, owing to a special relationship between the payer and the beneficial owner, or between both of them and some other person, the amount paid exceeds a normal commercial amount, the treaty exemption only applies to the commercial amount.

### *Independent activities*

The general position under Article 11 of the treaty is that a self-employed UK resident is not taxable in Australia in respect of activities carried out there unless he has a fixed base there regularly available to him.

### *Employment*

Article 12 of the treaty provides that where an individual performs services in Australia for an employer he will be subject to tax in Australia unless:

(1) he spends less than 183 days in Australia in the year to 30 June;
(2) the employer is not resident in Australia; and
(3) the remuneration is not deductible in computing the profits of a permanent establishment which the employer has in Australia.

### *Exceptions*

Article 13 of the treaty withdraws the benefits of Articles 11 and 12 as follows:

> 'Notwithstanding anything contained in Articles 11 and 12, income derived by public entertainers, such as theatre, motion picture, radio or television artistes, and musicians, and by athletes, from their personal activities as such shall be deemed to have a source in, and may be taxed in, the territory in which these activities are exercised.'

The provisions of this treaty are not as far-reaching as those of the UK/US treaty, and it would appear that, where an entertainer carries on his activities in Australia as an employee of a non-resident company, the exposure to Australian tax is limited to that on any salary paid to him and the rest of the profits may be accumulated in the company, providing that it does not have a permanent establishment in Australia and providing that the income earned by the company is not arising from or in relation to contracts or obligations to provide the services of public entertainers or artistes. Article 5(7)(c) will remove treaty protection from companies involved in providing the services of public entertainers and entertainers in some circumstances.

### *Tax rates*

These are shown in Appendix XI.

## France

### Domestic law

A French resident is generally subject to tax at rates up to 56.8% on all his income from all sources. Where, however, an individual becomes resident in France, there may be significant tax savings obtained from averaging provisions. These enable an individual to elect irrevocably for his income from artistic, literary or scientific works to be based on the average of the current year and either the preceding two or four years. Since, in the years preceding residence such income is nil, the first year's income would be reduced by two-thirds or four-fifths.

A person is considered resident in France if he meets any of the following conditions:

(1) it is the place where his family habitually lives;
(2) he spends more than 183 days a year in France;
(3) he exercises his profession principally in France;
(4) France is the centre of his economic interests.

A UK resident individual who is not resident in France is generally taxable on his income from French sources. This basic position is subject to the provisions of the UK/France double tax treaty. The modifications to the above position are set out below.

### Treaty relief

*Royalties*

Where royalties arise in France and are paid to a resident of the UK who is subject to tax there, they will only be taxable in the UK. No exemption is available where the UK resident has a permanent establishment in France with which the royalties are effectively connected.

The definition of 'royalty' for treaty purposes includes payments of any kind received as consideration for the use of, or the right to use, any copyright of literary, artistic or scientific work (including cinematograph films and films or tapes for radio or television broadcasting) and gains derived from the sale or exchange of rights or property giving rise to such royalties.

If, because of a special relationship between the payer and the recipient, or between both of them and some other person, the amount of royalty exceeds a normal commercial rate, then the excess over such a rate may be treated as a dividend or distribution.

*Independent activities*

The general position under Article 14 of the treaty is that a self-employed UK resident is not taxable in respect of activities carried out in France, provided he does not maintain a fixed base there. Where a fixed base is maintained, tax will be levied on the income accruing thereto.

*Employment*

Article 15 of the treaty provides that a UK citizen will not be taxed in respect of duties carried out in France under a contract of employment unless he spends more than 183 days in France and:

(1) his remuneration is paid by, or on behalf of, an employer resident in France; or
(2) the remuneration is borne by a permanent establishment or fixed base which his employer has in France.

*Exceptions*

Article 17 of the treaty withdraws the benefits of Articles 14 and 15 in the following circumstances:

> '(1) Notwithstanding the provisions of Articles 14 and 15, income derived by public entertainers, such as theatre, motion picture, radio or television artistes, and musicians, and by athletes, from their personal activities as such may be taxed in the Contracting State in which these activities are exercised.
> (2) Such income derived from the United Kingdom by a resident of France may also be taxed in France.'

Nevertheless, where a performer, resident or not, carries on his activities in France as an employee of a non-resident company, his exposure to tax may include all payments received by the non-resident company in so far as:

(1) the company is controlled, directly or indirectly, by the performer;
(2) its activities consist mainly in the rendering of services; or
(3) it is resident in a low-tax country.

In such a case, the performer is personally liable for French tax on the total amount received by the company, computed according to the rules applicable to the type of income involved.

*Tax rates*

These are shown in Appendix XI.

## Federal Republic of Germany

### Domestic law

A resident of Germany is taxable at rates up to 53% on all income from all sources. Church tax of 8 or 9% of the tax liability may be payable. The church tax depends on the federal state where the individual lives. From 1 January 1995 a surcharge of 7.5% of the total tax due will be levied.

An individual will be considered to be resident in Germany if that is either his domicile or customary place of abode.

The German concept of domicile differs from that used in the UK in that it depends on where a person resides on a more than temporary basis. Generally, an individual will be regarded as domiciled in Germany if he has a place of residence in Germany which he will retain and use.

A person is considered habitually resident in Germany if he has spent over six months in Germany with the purpose of generating income.

An individual who is not resident in Germany is subject to German tax on income from certain German sources.

### Treaty relief

The double tax treaty between the UK and Germany modifies this basic position and its general effect can be summarised as follows:

#### *Royalties*

Article VII provides that a royalty derived from sources within Germany by a UK resident who is subject to tax in the UK shall be taxable only in the UK. The exemption does not apply where the UK resident has a permanent establishment in Germany and the royalty is attributable to that establishment.

The definition of 'royalty' for the purposes of the treaty includes any royalty or other amount paid as consideration for the use of, or the privilege of using, any copyright of literary or artistic work, but does not include a rent or royalty paid in respect of cinematograph films.

Where a royalty between related parties exceeds a fair and reasonable rate, the excess is not covered by the treaty exemptions.

#### *Independent activities*

The general position under Article XI of the treaty is that income derived by a UK resident from services performed in Germany will only be taxable in Germany if he has a fixed base regularly available to him there.

#### *Employment*

The general position under Article XI of the treaty is that a UK resident is not liable to German tax on income earned from services performed in Germany unless:

(1) the individual is present in Germany for more than 183 days in the calendar year;
(2) the remuneration is paid by, or on behalf of, an employer who is a resident of Germany; or
(3) the remuneration is deducted from the profits of a fixed base which the employer has in Germany.

*Exceptions*

Paragraph 6 of Article XI withdraws the reliefs outlined above in respect of self-employed and employed individuals as follows:

> 'Notwithstanding anything contained in this Convention, income derived by public entertainers, such as theatre, motion picture, radio or television artistes, and musicians and by athletes, from their personal activities as such, may be taxed in the territory in which these activities are exercised.'

Again, this provision would only seem to give taxing rights in respect of income earned by performers, and the possibility of income accumulating in a company remains, provided the company does not have a permanent establishment in Germany.

*Tax rates*

These are shown in Appendix XI.

## The Netherlands

### Domestic law

Residents of The Netherlands are subject to tax at rates up to 60% in their worldwide income from all sources.

Non-residents are subject to tax on certain types of income derived from sources in The Netherlands. There is, however, a double tax treaty between the UK and The Netherlands which modifies the position.

Residence is determined by reference to an individual's personal facts and circumstances. Relevant factors include:

(1) the place of family residence;
(2) the maintenance of a house in The Netherlands (especially important in the absence of a residence elsewhere);
(3) the length of time spent in The Netherlands;
(4) membership of Dutch clubs, churches etc, and the type of school attended by his children;
(5) registration with the population registry;
(6) intention to reside in The Netherlands;
(7) the centre of his economic and social interests.

### Treaty relief

*Royalties*

Royalties derived and beneficially owned by a UK resident are only taxable in the UK.

The exemption from Netherlands tax is not available if the individual has a fixed base in The Netherlands with which the royalties are effectively connected.

Royalties for treaty purposes include payments of any kind received as consideration for the use of, or the right to use, any copyright of literary or artistic work including cinematograph films, and films or tapes for radio or television broadcasting.

Where, owing to a special relationship between the payer and the beneficial owner or both of them and some other person, the royalty exceeds a normal commercial rate, then the excess is not exempted by the treaty and may therefore lead to Netherlands taxation.

### *Independent activities*

The general position under Article 14 is that a UK resident is exempt from Netherlands tax in respect of services performed in The Netherlands provided he does not maintain a fixed base in that country.

### *Employment*

Article 15 provides that remuneration earned by a UK resident from an employment exercised in The Netherlands will be exempt from Netherlands tax unless:

(1) he spends more than 183 days in The Netherlands in the calendar year;
(2) the remuneration is paid by, or on behalf of, an employer who is resident in The Netherlands; or
(3) the remuneration is borne by a permanent establishment or fixed base which the employer has in The Netherlands.

### *Exceptions*

Article 17 of the treaty withdraws the reliefs for income from independent activities and employment outlined above in the following circumstances:

> '(1) Notwithstanding the provisions of Articles 14 and 15, income derived by a resident of one of the States as an entertainer, such as a theatre, motion picture, radio or television artiste, or a musician, or as an athlete, from his personal activities as such exercised in the other State, may be taxed in the other State.
> (2) Where income in respect of personal activities exercised by an entertainer or an athlete in his capacity as such accrues not to the entertainer or athlete himself but to another person, that income may, notwithstanding the provisions of Articles 7, 14 and 15, be taxed in the State in which the activities of the entertainer or athlete are exercised.'

Despite the wording of paragraph (2), Netherlands domestic legislation will not always permit the taxation of a non-resident performer.

Where the income from a short-term performance by a UK resident artiste is received either by himself or a non-Netherlands resident company with no fixed base in the Netherlands, Netherlands income tax may be limited to a flat withholding tax.

Where a longer term performance by an artiste is involved (generally more than three months) the income will be subject to normal Netherlands taxation.

UK resident athletes who perform in the Netherlands will generally be subject to Netherlands tax at the normal rates of taxation.

*Tax rates*

These are shown in Appendix XI.

## Republic of Ireland

### Domestic law

Residents of the Irish Republic are taxable at rates up to 48% (companies up to 40%) on their worldwide income with the exception of those residents who are not domiciled in the Republic, who are taxable on their income from Irish and UK sources and on any remittances of foreign income.

An individual will be deemed resident in Ireland if he meets any of the following tests:

(1) if he spends more than 183 days in the fiscal year (6 April to 5 April) in Ireland;
(2) if he habitually spends three months or more each year in Ireland;
(3) if he maintains a place of abode in Ireland and visits Ireland during the fiscal year; or
(4) if he goes to Ireland with the intention of taking up residence there for a number of years.

Non-residents are, in the absence of treaty relief, taxable at rates up to 48% on income from Irish sources.

Income levies are payable by resident individuals. The rates are 2.25% on income to a ceiling of £14,000 and 1% thereafter. Artists' exempt income (see p 163) is excluded in computing liability to these levies.

### Treaty relief

The treaty between the UK and the Republic of Ireland provides relief for UK residents receiving income from Ireland.

*Royalties*

Royalties derived and beneficially owned by a UK resident are only taxable in the United Kingdom. This exemption from Irish tax is not available if the individual has a fixed base in Ireland with which the royalties are effectively connected.

'Royalties' for treaty purposes include payments of any kind received as consideration for the use of, or right to use, any copyright of literary or artistic work including cinematograph films and films or tapes for radio or television broadcasting.

Where, owing to a special relationship between the payer and the beneficial owner or both of them and some other person, the royalty exceeds a normal commercial rate, then the excess is not exempted by the treaty.

### *Independent activities*

Where a UK resident performs independent services in Ireland, he will not be subject to Irish tax unless he maintains a permanent establishment in Ireland.

### *Employment*

Article 15 provides that emoluments earned by a UK resident in respect of an employment exercised in Ireland will be exempt from Irish tax unless:

(1) he spends more than 183 days in Ireland in the tax year (6 April to 5 April);
(2) the remuneration is borne by an employer who is resident in Ireland; or
(3) the remuneration is borne by a permanent establishment or fixed base which the employer has in Ireland.

### *Exceptions*

Article 16 of the treaty withdraws the reliefs outlined above as follows:

> '(1) Notwithstanding the provisions of Article 15, income derived by public entertainers, such as theatre, motion picture, radio or television artistes, and musicians, and by athletes, from their personal activities as such may be taxed in the Contracting State in which these activities are exercised.
>
> (2) Where income in respect of personal activities as such of an entertainer or athlete accrues not to that entertainer or athlete himself but to another person that income may, notwithstanding the provisions of Articles 8 and 15, be taxed in the Contracting State in which the activities of the entertainer or athlete are exercised.'

It can be seen that paragraph (2) prevents the accumulation of income in an employing company with the performer being paid a salary below the income actually generated in Ireland.

### *Other reliefs*

Irish domestic legislation (see Appendix X) provides an exemption from tax for profits or gains arising from the publication, production or sale of original and creative works, ie books or other writings, plays, musical compositions, paintings or sculptures, which the Revenue Commissioners determine to be of cultural or artistic merit. The exemption is available to individuals resident solely in Ireland who have written, either solely or jointly with another individual, composed or executed the work.

The extent to which relief is available for certain activities, eg record production, is uncertain and it is advisable to obtain written confirmation of the availability of the relief from the tax authorities.

*Tax rates*

These are shown in Appendix XI.

## Japan

**Domestic law**

Permanent residents of Japan are taxable on their worldwide income.

Non-permanent residents are taxable on income from Japanese sources and any foreign income paid in, or remitted to, Japan. Non-permanent residents are normally individuals who have lived continuously in Japan for over a year but for less than five years.

Non-residents are generally taxable only on income derived from Japan.

**Treaty relief**

This basic position is modified by the UK/Japan double tax treaty as outlined below.

*Royalties*

Royalties arising in Japan and beneficially owned by a UK resident may be taxed in Japan at a rate not exceeding 10% of the gross amount of the royalties.

This reduction in the rate of withholding tax is not available if the UK resident has a permanent establishment in Japan with which the royalties are connected.

'Royalties' for the purpose of the treaty include payments of any kind received as a consideration for the use of, or the right to use, any copyright of literary or artistic work, including cinematograph films, and films or tapes for radio or television broadcasting.

In addition, this relief extends to proceeds arising from the alienation of any copyright of literary or artistic work including cinematograph films.

Where, because of a special relationship between the payer and the beneficial owner of the royalties or between both of them and some other person, the royalties exceed a normal commercial rate, then the excess will not be eligible for treaty relief.

*Independent activities*

Income derived by a UK resident from activities in Japan is exempt from tax in Japan under Article 15, unless he maintains a fixed base in Japan.

*Employment*

Income derived by a resident of the UK from the exercise of his employment in Japan is exempt from Japanese tax unless:

(1) he spends more than 183 days in a calendar year in Japan;
(2) the remuneration is paid by, or on behalf of, an employer who is a resident of Japan; or
(3) the remuneration is borne by a permanent establishment or a fixed base which the employer has in Japan.

*Exceptions*

Article 18 of the treaty amends the position outlined above as follows:

> 'Notwithstanding the provisions of Articles 15 and 16, income derived by public entertainers, such as theatre, motion picture, radio or television artistes, and musicians, and by athletes, from their personal activities as such may be taxed in the Contracting State in which these activities are exercised.'

This, in conjunction with Japanese domestic legislation, allows Japan to levy a tax of 20% on the individual's Japanese source income.

Although, prima facie, this provision does not preclude the use of a Japanese resident employing company to accumulate income without suffering a charge to Japanese tax, Article 6(4) provides that a company providing the services of entertainers or athletes shall be deemed to have a permanent establishment in Japan.

*Tax rates*

These are shown in Appendix XI.

# Appendix IX
# Relevant double taxation provisions

Set out below is a list of countries with which the UK has double tax agreements, the type of 'artiste and athlete' articles contained in each agreement and the rate of withholding tax on royalties.

## Type 1

Articles which do not allow the domestic tax authority the power to 'look through' the legal relationship between employer and employee when restricting treaty benefits.

## Type 2

Articles which allow the domestic authority to 'look through' the employee/employer relationship for treaty purposes. The fact that the treaty permits this does not mean that the domestic legislation actually has the means to do so.

| | | *Type of clause* | | *Royalty withholding* | |
|---|---|---|---|---|---|
| *Country* | *1* | *2* | *None* | *rates* | *Note* |
| Antigua | * | | | Nil | |
| Australia | * | | | 10% | 1 |
| Austria | * | | | Nil | 2 |
| Bangladesh | | * | | 10% | 3 |
| Barbados | * | | | Nil | |
| Belgium | | * | | Nil | |
| Belize | * | | | Nil | |
| Botswana | * | | | 15% | |
| Brunei | * | | | Nil | |
| Bulgaria | | * | | Nil | |
| Burma | * | | | Nil | |
| Canada | | * | | Nil | |
| China | | * | | 10% | |
| Cyprus | * | | | Nil | 4 |
| Denmark | | * | | Nil | 5 |
| Dominica | * | | | Nil | |

| *Country* | *Type of clause* 1 | 2 | *None* | *Royalty withholding rates* | *Note* |
|---|---|---|---|---|---|
| Egypt | | * | | 15% | |
| Falkland Islands | | * | | Nil | |
| Faroe Islands | * | | | Nil | |
| Fiji | * | | | 15% | 6 |
| Finland | | * | | Nil | |
| France | * | | | Nil | |
| The Gambia | | | * | 12.5% | |
| Germany | * | | | Nil | |
| Ghana | * | | | Nil | |
| Greece | * | | | Nil | |
| Grenada | * | | | Nil | |
| Guernsey | * | | | Nil | |
| Guyana | | * | | 10% | |
| Hungary | * | | | Nil | 7 |
| Iceland | | * | | Nil | 8 |
| India | | * | | 30% | |
| Indonesia | * | | | 10% | |
| Irish Republic | | * | | Nil | |
| Isle of Man | * | | | Nil | |
| Israel | * | | | 15% | 3 |
| Italy | | * | | 8% | |
| Ivory Coast | | * | | 10% | |
| Jamaica | * | | | 10% | |
| Japan | | * | | 10% | |
| Jersey | * | | | Nil | |
| Kenya | * | | | 15% | |
| Kiribati & Tuvalu | * | | | Nil | |
| Korea | | * | | 15% | |
| Lesotho | * | | | Nil | |
| Luxemburg | * | | | 5% | 8 |
| Malawi | * | | | Nil | |
| Malaysia | * | | | 15% | |
| Malta | * | | | Nil | |
| Mauritius | | * | | 15% | |
| Montserrat | * | | | Nil | |
| Morocco | | * | | 10% | |
| Namibia | * | | | Nil | 9 |
| Netherlands | | * | | Nil | |
| Nethds Antilles | * | | | Nil | |
| New Zealand | | * | | 10% | |
| Nigeria | | * | | 12.5% | |
| Norway | | * | | Nil | |
| Pakistan | | * | | 12.5% | |
| Papua New Guinea | | * | | 10% | |
| Philippines | | * | | 25% | 10 |
| Poland | | * | | 10% | |
| Portugal | * | | | 5% | |
| Romania | * | | | 10% | |
| St Kitts & Nevis | * | | | Nil | |
| St Lucia | * | | | Nil | |
| St Vincent | * | | | Nil | |
| Seychelles | * | | | Nil | |
| Sierra Leone | * | | | Nil | |

| Country | Type of clause 1 | 2 | None | Royalty withholding rates | Note |
|---|---|---|---|---|---|
| Singapore | * | | | 15% | 11 |
| Solomon Islands | * | | | Nil | |
| South Africa | * | | | Nil | |
| Spain | | * | | 10% | |
| Sri Lanka | | * | | 10% | |
| Sudan | * | | | 10% | |
| Swaziland | | * | | Nil | |
| Sweden | | * | | Nil | |
| Switzerland | | * | | Nil | |
| Thailand | | * | | 5% | 12 |
| Trinidad & Tobago | * | | | 10% | 13 |
| Tunisia | | * | | 15% | |
| Turkey | | * | | 10% | |
| Uganda | | * | | 15% | |
| Ukraine | | * | | Nil | |
| USSR | | * | | Nil | 14/15 |
| USA | | * | | Nil | 16 |
| Yugoslavia | | * | | 10% | |
| Zambia | * | | | 10% | |
| Zimbabwe | | * | | 10% | |

*Notes*

(1) See page 150 regarding the nature of the artiste and athlete clause.
(2) Royalty withholding of 10% if UK company holds more than 50% of voting power in payer.
(3) Royalties for film and TV rights are subject to withholding tax based on the application of local corporation tax rates to 15% of the gross royalty.
(4) 5% for film royalties.
(5) Contains anti-treaty 'shopping' clause.
(6) Copyright royalties (not cinematic) – nil.
(7) The first £8,000 of gross receipts are not taxed in Hungary.
(8) Film royalties – 12%.
(9) Film royalties – 5%.
(10) 15% for film and television royalties.
(11) 30% for film and television royalties.
(12) 15% for film or television royalties.
(13) Nil for literary, dramatic, musical and artistic work.
(14) Currently applies to Russian Federation, Armenia, Azerbarjan, Kazokhstan, Moldeva, Tajikistan, Turkmenistan, Uzbekistan, Georgia and Belarrue.
(15) Entertainers taxed only in country of residence.
(16) Performing income exempt if receipts do not exceed US$15,000 in the year.

# Appendix X
# Republic of Ireland
# FA 1969

The Finance Act 1969, s 2 provides that income from works of artistic merit, which would otherwise be assessable under Case II of Schedule D, is to be disregarded for all purposes of the Income Tax Acts in the case of assessments for the year 1969/70 and subsequent years.

For the exemption to apply, the following requirements must be satisfied:

(1) The income must be income of an individual resident in the Republic of Ireland and not resident elsewhere.
(2) The income must arise from an original and creative work having cultural or artistic merit and being:
 (a) a book or other writing;
 (b) a play;
 (c) a musical composition;
 (d) a painting or like picture; or
 (e) a sculpture.
(3) The decision as to whether or not the work has cultural or artistic merit is one for the Revenue Commissioners after such consultation (if any) as they deem necessary with such person or body of persons as they think may be of assistance to them.
(4) A claim may be in respect of a work executed before or after the passing of the Act and may be made for a joint work as well as one executed by the individual solely.
(5) The exemption will not apply to an assessment for any year prior to the year of assessment in which the claim is made.
(6) The individual must submit to the Revenue Commissioners such evidence as they require to determine the claim including books, accounts and documents relating to the publication, production or sale of the work and, to determine the amount to be exempted, the Revenue Commissioners may make such apportionment of receipts and expenses as may be necessary.
(7) In the case of books, writings, plays or musical compositions, the claimant must submit three copies to the Revenue Commissioners and, in the case of paintings or sculptures, the individual must provide such facilities as the Revenue Commissioners think necessary from the person who owns or has in his possession the painting, picture or sculpture.

In the course of the debate on the Finance Bill, the then Hon Minister for Finance, Mr Haughey, stated it would not normally be necessary to examine all the works of the writer, composer, artist or sculptor and that, normally, if one of the individual's works was deemed to have cultural or artistic merit, all the works of that individual in that field would be exempt. He expected that persons who had already won general recognition in their spheres of endeavour would qualify for the tax exemption on their reputation and that only a minority would be required to submit their work to the Revenue Commissioners.

# Appendix XI
# Overseas tax rates

## United States

A non-resident alien engaged in a trade, including employment, in the US is eligible for a personal exemption of US$2,350 and the balance of his taxable income, for the year to 31 December 1993, is taxable as follows:

*Single individuals*

| Taxable income Over | But not over | Pay | Rate on excess | Of the amount over |
|---|---|---|---|---|
| US$ | US$ | US$ | % | US$ |
| 0 | 22,100 | 0 | 15 | 0 |
| 22,100 | 53,500 | 3,315 | 28 | 22,100 |
| 53,500 | 115,000 | 12,107 | 31 | 53,500 |
| 115,000 | 250,000 | 31,172 | 36 | 115,000 |
| 250,000 | - | 79,772 | 39.6 | 250,000 |

*Married individuals submitting separate returns (non-resident aliens cannot use married filing joint status)*

| Taxable income Over | But not over | Pay | Rate on excess | Of the amount over |
|---|---|---|---|---|
| US$ | US$ | US$ | % | US$ |
| 0 | 18,450 | 0 | 15 | 0 |
| 18,450 | 44,575 | 2,767.50 | 28 | 18,450 |
| 44,575 | 70,000 | 10,082.50 | 31 | 44,575 |
| 70,000 | 125,000 | 17,964.25 | 36 | 70,000 |
| 125,000 | - | 37,764.25 | 39.6 | 125,000 |

The benefit of the personal exemption is phased out where income exceeds US$108,450 (single) and US$81,350 (married filing separately).

# Australia

Husband and wife are treated as separate taxpayers. The rates in force and proposed for Australian residents for the years ending 30 June 1994 are:

### Resident individuals

| *Taxable income* | *Tax* | *Rates on excess* |
|---|---|---|
| $A | $A | % |
| 5,400 | Nil | 20 |
| 20,700 | 3,060 | 35.33 |
| 36,000 | 8,465 | 38 |
| 38,000 | 9,225 | 44 |
| 50,000 | 14,505 | 47 |

Excludes 1.4% Medicare levy.

### Non-resident individuals

| *Taxable income* | *Tax* | *Rates on excess* |
|---|---|---|
| $A | $A | % |
| 0 | Nil | 29 |
| 20,700 | 6,003 | 35.33 |
| 36,000 | 11,408 | 38 |
| 38,000 | 12,168 | 44 |
| 50,000 | 17,448 | 47 |

# France

The rates in force for the calendar year 1994, based on income for 1993, per 'family part' are:

| *Taxable income* | *Marginal rate* | *Cumulative tax* |
|---|---|---|
| FF | % | FF |
| 0–21,900 | 0 | 0 |
| | | 3,120 |
| 47,900–84,300 | 25 | 12,220 |
| 84,300–136,500 | 35 | 30,490 |
| 136,500–222,100 | 45 | 69,010 |
| 222,100–273,900 | 50 | 94,910 |

*Notes*

(1) The tax reductions arising from the split income system are limited to FF15,600 per half a part over 1 for a single taxpayer and over 2 for a married couple.

(2) For non-residents, the tax liability cannot be less than 25% of the net taxable income from French sources.

(3) A surcharge of 2.6% will be levied on the income of French residents.

## Federal Republic of Germany

Tax is determined by the use of official tax tables that contain minutely graduated tax brackets. However, the following table shows the tax burden on representative income levels for the tax (calendar) year 1994.

| *Taxable income* | *Single* | *Married* |
|---|---|---|
| DM | DM | DM |
| 10,000 | 836 | 0 |
| 20,000 | 2,943 | 1,672 |
| 30,000 | 5,354 | 3,692 |
| 40,000 | 8,067 | 5,886 |
| 50,000 | 11,084 | 8,208 |
| 100,000 | 30,743 | 22,168 |
| 160,000 | 61,930 | 43,954 |
| 200,000 | 83,137 | 61,486 |

## The Netherlands

### Residents

The resident individual income tax rates applying for the 1994 year are as follows:

| *Taxable income* | *Tax rates* |
|---|---|
| Dfl | % |
| less than 43,267 | 7.05[1] |
| 43,267–86,532 | 50 |
| more than 86,532 | 60 |

[1] The 7.05% rate is usually quoted as 38.25%, because all taxpayers under 65 pay a 31.2% social security contribution on the same band of income.

All taxpayers are entitled to a standard deduction (personal allowance) of Dfl 5,952 in 1994.

### Non-residents

| *Taxable income* | *Tax rates* |
|---|---|
| Dfl | % |
| less than 43,267 | 25 |
| 43,267–86,532 | 50 |
| more than 86,532 | 60 |

The 25% rate applies to non-residents who are not subject to Dutch social security and whose Dutch income is less than 90% of their total worldwide income. Under certain conditions the rate of the first bracket can be less than 25%. This rate will be reduced further to 7.05% where a non-resident's Dutch taxable income exceeds 90% of his or her total worldwide income. It is required, however, that the individual concerned be subject to a non-Dutch social security system.

## Republic of Ireland

Personal allowances of IR£2,350 for a single person and IR£4,700 for married persons jointly assessed are available.

Rates in force for the year ending 5 April 1995:

| *Single* | *Married jointly assessed* | *Marginal rate* |
|---|---|---|
| IR£ | IR£ | % |
| 1–8,200 | 1–16,400 | 27 |
| 8,201 upwards | 16,401 upwards | 48 |

## Japan

Residents (permanent and non-permanent) are subject to both income tax and inhabitants' tax. The inhabitants' tax rates can vary from city to city and are applied to the previous year's taxable income (as marginally adjusted).

Rates in force for the calendar year 1993:

### National income tax

| *Taxable income* | | *Tax on* | *Rate on* |
|---|---|---|---|
| *Exceeding* | *Not exceeding* | *lower amount* | *excess* |
| Y | Y | Y | % |
| 0 | 3,000,000 | 0 | 10 |
| 3,000,000 | 6,000,000 | 300,000 | 20 |
| 6,000,000 | 10,000,000 | 900,000 | 30 |
| 10,000,000 | 20,000,000 | 2,100,000 | 40 |
| 20,000,000 | - | 6,100,000 | 50 |

### Inhabitants' tax

The following tables show how the two components of inhabitants' tax are calculated.

## *Per capita levy*

MUNICIPAL INHABITANT TAX

| | *Standard* | *Maximum* | *Prefectural inhabitant tax* |
|---|---|---|---|
| | Y | Y | Y |
| Cities with a population of 500,000 or more | 2,500 | 3,200 | 700 |
| Cities with a population of 50,000 to 500,000 | 2,000 | 2,600 | 700 |
| Other municipalities | 1,500 | 2,000 | 700 |

## Income levy

MUNICIPAL TAX

| *Taxable income* | | *Tax on lower amount* | *Rate on excess* |
|---|---|---|---|
| *Exceeding* | *Not exceeding* | | |
| Y | Y | Y | % |
| 0 | 1,600,000 | 0 | 3 |
| 1,600,000 | 5,500,000 | 48,000 | 8 |
| 5,500,000 | | 360,000 | 11 |

PREFECTURAL TAX

| *Taxable income* | | *Tax on lower amount* | *Rate on excess* |
|---|---|---|---|
| *Exceeding* | *Not exceeding* | | |
| Y | Y | Y | % |
| 0 | 5,500,000 | 0 | 2 |
| 5,500,000 | | 110,000 | 4 |

Where the entertainer is non-resident, he is subject to 20% withholding tax on gross income and inhabitants' tax is not charged.

# Appendix XII The place of supply rules for services provided by performers and ancillary services involved in staging a performance in the EC

| | | Belgium | Denmark | France | Germany | Greece | Ireland | Italy | Luxembourg | Netherlands | Portugal | Spain | UK |
|---|---|---|---|---|---|---|---|---|---|---|---|---|---|
| 1. | REGISTRATION | | | | | | | | | | | | |
| | Performer | Yes | Yes | Yes | Yes(3) | Yes(3) | Yes | Yes(3) | Yes | Yes(3) | Yes(3) | Yes(3) | Yes |
| | Booking Agent | No(7) | No(7) | No(7) | No(7) | No(7) | No(7) | No(7) | No(7) | No(7) | No(7) | No(7) | No(7) |
| | PA System Service | Yes | Yes | Yes | Yes(3) | Yes(3) | Yes | Yes(3) | Yes | Yes(3) | Yes(3) | Yes(3) | Yes |
| | Road Crew | Yes | Yes | Yes | Yes(3) | Yes(3) | Yes | Yes(3) | Yes | Yes(3) | Yes(3) | Yes(3) | Yes |
| | Management Agents | No(1) | No(1) | No(1) | No(1) | No(1) | No(1) | No(1) | No(1) | No(1) | No(1) | No(1) | No(1) |
| | Advertising | No(2) | No(2) | No(2) | No(2) | No(2) | No(2) | No(2) | No(2) | No(2) | No(2) | No(2) | No(2) |
| 2. | Turnover Limit | Nil | DK10,000 | Nil | DM25,000 | DR250,000 | Nil | Nil | LFrs400,000 | DFL2172 | ESC500,000 | Nil | £45,000 |
| | (Sterling) | | (£1,000) | | (£10,000) | (800) | | | (6,800) | (£700) | (£2,000) | | |
| 3. | Rate of VAT | 6% | 25% | 5.5% or 18.6% | 15% | 18% | 12.5% | 19% | 15% | 18.5% | 17% | 15% | 17.5% |

| . | | Belgium | Denmark | France | Germany | Greece | Ireland | Italy | Luxembourg | Netherlands | Portugal | Spain | UK |
|---|---|---|---|---|---|---|---|---|---|---|---|---|---|
| 4. | Is it necessary to have an establishment in the Member State? | No | No | No | No | No | No | No | No | No | No | No | No |
| 5. | VAT Shift to recipient facility if there is no establishment | | | | | | | | | | | | |
| | On a one-off basis | Yes(2) | No(2) | Yes | Yes | Yes | No(4) | Yes | No | Yes | Yes | Yes | Yes(4) |
| | On an on-going basis | No | No(2) | Yes | Yes | Yes | No(4) | Yes | No | Yes | Yes | Yes | Yes(4) |
| 6. | Is a tax representative necessary if no VAT shift facility is available and there is no establishment? | Yes | Yes | Yes | Yes | Yes | No | No | Yes | No | No(5) | No(5) | No(5&6) |

*Notes*

(1) The supply of such services, takes place 'when received' in that the recipient, if VAT registered, accounts for the tax. If the recipient is not in business the supplier must charge VAT at the rate due in their own Member State.

(2) Certain supplies have the VAT liability shifted to the recipient.

(3) The supplier only has to register if it has an establishment in the Member State which includes having an agent there.

(4) A non-resident business can register at its address outside the Member State and does not have to appoint a tax representative.

(5) If a tax representative is appointed, it will have a joint liability for the supplier's tax.

(6) The appointment of a tax representative is optional.

(7) See comments in text under 'Supply'.

# Index